C000193885

# Summary Bunc

# Love | Readtrepreneur

# Publishing: Includes Summary

# of Living with a SEAL &

# Summary of Love and Respect

## ABBEY BEATHAN

**Text Copyright © ABBEY BEATHAN**

All rights reserved. No part of this guide may be reproduced
in any form without permission in writing from the publisher
except in the case of brief quotations embodied in critical
articles or reviews.

## Legal & Disclaimer

The information contained in this book is not designed to replace or take the place of any form of medicine or professional medical advice. The information in this book has been provided for educational and entertainment purposes only.

The information contained in this book has been compiled from sources deemed reliable, and it is accurate to the best of the Author's knowledge; however, the Author cannot guarantee its accuracy and validity and cannot be held liable for any errors or omissions. Changes are periodically made to this book. You must consult your doctor or get professional medical advice before using any of the suggested remedies, techniques, or information in this book. Images used in this book are not the same as of that of the actual book. This is a totally separate and different entity from that of the original book titled: "Living with a SEAL"

Upon using the information contained in this book, you agree to hold harmless the Author from and against any damages, costs, and expenses, including any legal fees potentially resulting from the application of any of the information provided by this guide.

This disclaimer applies to any damages or injury caused by the use and application, whether directly or indirectly, of any advice or information presented, whether for breach of contract, tort, negligence, personal injury, criminal intent, or under any other cause of action.

You agree to accept all risks of using the information presented inside this book. You need to consult a professional medical practitioner in order to ensure you are both able and healthy enough to participate in this program.

# Table of Contents

# The Book at a Glance

Jesse Itzler wants to spice up his life. He wants to become a better person so that he can live a better life. A life full of excitement and surprises. To achieve this, he decides that he must get into shape. However, he cannot do this alone, so he asks a Navy soldier who goes by the name SEAL, to guide him. He first saw SEAL during a warm-up before a relay race where he himself was participating in. He described SEAL to standout because he always had a stern, unwelcoming expression on his face. He was sitting like a statue, looking straight instead of warming-up like the rest of the participants. Unlike everyone who had first-aid kits and packed lunches, he had nothing but a box of crackers and water. During the race, Itzler was observing SEAL. His spirit and sense of determination is what told Itzler that he could be the one to change his life, forever.

To Itzler, SEAL was the ideal version that he wanted to become. If you were to ignore his intimidating, off-limits nature, you would find that he could be the perfect teacher—and possibly even the perfect friend. Not to mention, his body is of pure muscle, which shows that he is not a joke but the real deal. Therefore, he took the liberty of inviting SEAL to live in his home as his trainer. That is where his progression to a better life, began. He entered a world he never thought existed. He met someone who could do things he thought were mentally and physically impossible. Moreover, that "someone" is going to train him to do the impossible.

His first encounters with SEAL were—crazy. SEAL did not smile very often and seemed to have no sense of humour. He barely responded to Itzler's questions and when he did, gave some cold statements. It was a quite a struggle for Itzler to keep up with SEAL, sometimes. Training was extreme and Itzler felt excruciating pain.

During the time that they spent together, Itzler starts to understand SEAL's reason for being the way he is and SEAL opens up, little by little. Before the two had met, they were living lives that were very different from each other. Therefore, it really was a struggle to become fond of each other, at the beginning. Both men were missing something. Apparently, one had what the other did not have. They completed each other by sharing their differences.

Itzler's experience of living with SEAL was torturous at the beginning, yet he was able to endure it all. Initially, he was already living a good life—he did not need to become better. His sense of obligation to improve made his life a good one. He is a good person in the sense that he always does his best. He accepts that he needs to feel pain to gain the knowledge he craves. He wants to learn—to the extent that he is literally bleeding from the gained experience. The pain that Itzler was experiencing was indeed horrifying to all. Who would want to experience that much pain? SEAL's training is somewhat discouraging, but this book proved that it is accurate. The results that Itzler ended up with proved that there is no gain without pain. You cannot move forward if you are too afraid to put your foot forward.

It takes a strong man to be able to absorb all those experiences without going mad. If a human is forced to do something he does not want to do, that affects their mental state in a bad way—no matter how mentally healthy a human is. It is human nature. Jesse Itzler was strong enough to suppress those urges to run away—to quit. He was strong enough to maintain his character—while improving it. He did not break, as most people do.

The book displays that there is one thing that a human must do to achieve a good life. The one thing that a human cannot choose not to do is to experience hardship. How did the greats, become "greats"? How did the wise, become "wise"? They did two things that were unavoidable; they made a mistake and they learned from it. They had no choice but to learn from their mistakes so that they would not experience it again. The more painful a mistake was, the more meaningful the lesson is. Perhaps that is what has been going through SEAL's mind.

SEAL is quite different from a normal person. He stares at walls and is able to do absolutely nothing at all, for long periods. He is almost similar to a robot—a statue, if you may, when he is idle. We later learn that this is what enables him to go into some "hero" mode. He is able to foretell an outcome based on everything he can observe. This may require him to be more attentive and he may need to use his senses for this purpose. It is difficult to be careless yet careful at the same time. It is probably impossible. No human possesses such abilities.

Although he has a sense of humour and he is not heartless, he is always looking cold. This may be the downside of staying cool and dependable. It is clear that he can be quite a softy depending on the situation. It is safe to say that SEAL is a human with great, hard-earned abilities.

# PROLOGUE

In December 2010, a man who goes by the name SEAL moved into Jesse Itzler's home, to be his trainer. It was a very inconvenient time of the year due to unfit weather conditions. For this reason, Itzler was almost certain that his plans with SEAL would fall into shambles. Apparently, that was not a part of SEAL's plan.

# Chapter 1: The Arrival

It is early in the morning and Jesse Itzler is in his home with his wife, Sara and his son, Lazer. He is awaiting the arrival of SEAL. Itzler is excited and nervous to begin his training, thoughts racing through his head.

He first saw SEAL at a relay race. SEAL stood-out from the rest of the participants because of his intimidating yet simple appearance. Itzler thought that he would be great trainer material. He personally gave SEAL his regards and invited him to stay in his home, to help him get into better physical and mental shape. SEAL agreed to his proposal, with only one condition; that Itzler does everything he is told to do, without resistance and/or complaints. SEAL assured him that he would get outstanding results when their training is complete. Itzler reluctantly agreed. As a result, a bargain exists.

SEAL arrived at the exact time he said he would arrive. He seemed to have no personal belongings with him. He was not even dressed appropriately for the weather. SEAL did not even greet his trainee. Nevertheless, Itzler welcomed him. He tried using some expressions to make SEAL feel truly welcome. Instead, SEAL gave him cold and harsh responses. He made it clear that he did not do well with expressions. Itzler did not argue and just went with what SEAL wanted.

They started their training with a piece of advice that SEAL gave to Itzler. Itzler found his advice to be little weird and unrealistic. However, he thought that this was just a phase to getting closer to SEAL. At some point, he wanted to keep their conversation going, so he asked some questions. The answers that SEAL gave him, did not do much to satisfy him.

The first thing they do is run six miles to Central Park, at a fast pace. Itzler was thinking that SEAL wanted to test his abilities by making him go at this speed. This was difficult for Itzler because speed was not his strength—it was his ability to run for long periods. For him, it was better to be able to talk to someone while at the same time running. Even though it was difficult, he just accepted the challenge saying it was good for him.

After freshening up, Itzler showed SEAL around his home. He began by teaching SEAL how to use the television and where the eating utensils were. SEAL found none of these relevant. When they go into the laundry room, SEAL decides that he had seen enough and demanded that they go to the gym.

At the gym, SEAL seems to be showing more enthusiasm. He gives a little smile when they entered, and the smile grew wider when he tested a pull-up bar. He states that the bar is perfect and that Itzler should start right away. He commanded him to do ten, so that he can witness his abilities. Itzler immediately jumps up and grabs the bar. He was close to reaching ten when he gave up and dropped down. SEAL tells him to take rest for a bit and repeat his command. Itzler breathes and does the same thing again, but does not improve. He repeats and reaches 17 pull-ups in separate attempts. He decided that he has had enough, and requests that they go home. With an emotionless expression, SEAL tells him that they are not going back until he does a hundred pull-ups. After some protesting, Itzler has no choice but to obey. It took a while, but he managed to achieve a hundred pull-ups.

Today, he ran six miles and did a hundred pull-ups.

# No Novocain

Jesse Itzler grew up on Long Island in Roslyn, New York. He is the youngest of three siblings. He had a suburban environment. He has a loving mother. At the same time, she was quite stern. On the part of discipline, it seemed to be the mother's call. His father was more of the cool type. He would always be present for the important events of their lives. He owns a plumbing supply store. His hobby is something like a mad scientist. He enjoyed creating things in the basement. Once, he even made a cool project for Jesse.

His mother did not approve of the use of X-rays, fluoride, and Novocain. Even though his father has no problem with ay of these, they are all off-limits. Jesse Itzler knew this was off-limits as long as he is living with his mother. Trips to the dentist were more painful compared to the visits of kids who use Novocain and did not have a crazy dentist. Itzler did not have pleasant memories of his childhood dentist.

# Chapter 2: Nature's Gatorade

It was extremely difficult for Itzler to sleep due to his sore muscles. This made him realize that he will have to work harder to gain SEAL's approval. His crazy workout on the first day told him a lot about SEAL; that he is serious. SEAL has high expectations with him.

Itzler is to wake up because of the alarm clock SEAL ordered him to set. Even before the alarm clock could do its job, SEAL went ahead and made some seemingly accidental noises to wake Itzler up 30 minutes before the actual time he was to wake. This annoyed Itzler, but he got up anyway.

They do the same running pace as yesterday. The vibe between them was just as silent and cold as it was yesterday. It was then that Itzler thought that he had low chances of forming a friendly bond with SEAL, as he was very distant and mysterious. They did not seem to like each other. Time seemed to be flowing rather slowly and Itzler was more uncomfortable around SEAL than he was the first time.

Itzler had a meeting regarding business and he had to go to Boston. He wants to promote the brand Zico Coconut

Water. He had easily forgotten to announce this to SEAL because he was thinking that it would not do much harm, because of the fact that it was work-related. Later, Itzler invited SEAL to come with him. At first, SEAL was not very happy with the last-minute plan, but he agreed to tag along. Itzler assured him that they would be back early tonight so that they can still train.

It was an exciting event for Itzler because he would be meeting Boston Celtic's legendary basketball player, Kevin Garnett. Although it did not do much to make SEAL excited. Garnett is an official endorser for Gatorade, but at the same time enjoys Zico. Itzler was thinking that it would be convenient for the legend to leave Gatorade for Zico.

The two travel to Boston by jet. Ironically, Itzler who began a private jet company is not much of a flyer. Amazingly, SEAL does not seem to be bothered. He is able to read and relax. He was able to keep his usual straight face all through the flight.

They land and head over to the meeting room. There was Kevin Garnett and his financial team. Itzler shakes Garnett's hand and greets him, but it seems Garnett is stunned when he saw SEAL. Itzler introduced SEAL and explained what the situation was. Garnett is still stunned. All through the meeting, Garnett's attention was on SEAL. He was interviewing SEAL about workouts. It was cool to watch, but sort of left Itzler out. The meeting was over—without a single word about Zico. In that time, it seemed Garnett and SEAL had formed a bond. Garnett also wanted SEAL to train him.

SEAL seemed to be in a better mood than usual, because he fist bumped Itzler as they walked out of the building. Their happy moment died instantly when they walked into a snowsquall as soon as they went through the doors. They decided it was better to check into a hotel near Boston Garden.

Itzler's initial plan was to relax in his room, but that was hushed when SEAL knocked on his door and announced that they were going to run, in these conditions. It is the second run for today and Itzler is not even prepared to do this.

When they got back to the hotel, Itzler was not very happy as he nearly got a frostbite. His clothes are soaking wet. He tried to call and update Sara, but it seemed like she was already asleep. He knew she always goes to sleep early. The first time he met her, he thought she was weird. He ended up marrying her.

Itzler just left a message for Sara in the voicemail. He just hoped for the best when the sun rises tomorrow.

Today, he went 12 miles in a small blizzard.

# Chapter 3: My Nuts

The ringing of the hotel phone woke Itzler up. Unsurprisingly, it was SEAL on the other end of the line. It was inconvenient for Itzler to have spent the night in Boston, as he had no change of clothes. Unfortunately, his clothes from yesterday had not dried up. He tried to bring the problem up with SEAL, hoping that he might sympathize. Sadly, this did not move SEAL—not one bit. Itzler was not even lucky enough to be able to use his underwear.

Bad luck did not end there. It was still dark outside because it was around five in the morning. SEAL told Itzler to keep up with him, which was extremely difficult because he was going fast. He was also running dangerously close to moving cars. Itzler did not enjoy any of it.

When it was time to turn around, the sun was half-awake. Since Itzler was not so concentrated on dodging the vehicles anymore, he started to feel the excruciating pain of the fabric of his shorts rubbing vigorously on his nuts. The friction burn was so bad that it even bled. Even so, SEAL told him to maintain the pace. They did not run back straight to the hotel. SEAL was finding every path to take that would extend their running period. When they reached 8.3 miles, they were back at the hotel and SEAL was satisfied.

Three hours later, Itzler calls SEAL and suggests that they get to the airport. The flights were delayed for quite some time. They were forced to just sit and wait at the airport. All the while, Itzler was observing SEAL. He concluded that he really was no regular human being. While Itzler could not stand doing nothing, SEAL did absolutely nothing at all.

SEAL tells Itzler to get ready for their three miles. Itzler was tired, but he did not dare protest, as SEAL seemed to be more angry than usual.

During the whole run, SEAL did not look at his GPS once. Amazingly, he still knew exactly how many miles they were going. Itzler was just thinking that SEAL is amazing.

Itzler still has not quite formed a bond with SEAL, but he felt that it was good to acknowledge him as a friend. When he goes to SEAL's room to call it a night, SEAL tells Itzler to get the most uncomfortable chair and a blanket, and sleep on it. Itzler could not believe what SEAL was telling him to do—neither did his supportive wife. Nevertheless, he did try to sleep on that uncomfortable chair.

Today, they did fourteen point three miles.

# Sara's First Sighting

Sara had seen SEAL in a one hundred thirty-five-mile ultra-marathon called the Badwater race. Jesse had wanted to join that marathon, but she was reluctant on letting him go. She suggested that they go and watch the race beforehand to convince Jesse that the idea was crazy. The whole idea was insanity. Known as the toughest races in history, because it goes through the Mojave Desert's Death Valley in a shaded area of one hundred thirty degrees. It is certain that there is a significant reason for calling it "Death Valley".

Sara's first encounter with SEAL did not seem pleasant as he ignored her when she cheered for him. Who ever thought that that same man would be living in their house, as a trainer?

# Chapter 4: Fitness Test

Itzler did not sleep continuously. If combined, it would be equivalent to a maximum of two hours of sleep. Even though his night was torture, SEAL never brought it up or showed the least bit of concern.

Now SEAL wants to test if Itzler has developed a solid "base". They head downstairs to the gym. When they got there, SEAL removed his shirt and analysed himself in the mirror. When Itzler told him that it is against the rules, SEAL says that the rule is stupid. He is slightly showing a little more "human" in him.

The intense fitness training begins with pull-ups and push-ups. Itzler is still having a difficult time keeping up. SEAL tests Itzler on the treadmill and box jump. On all the activities, SEAL is taking notes on Itzler's performance.

Itzler feels that it is amazing that SEAL is doing almost every single workout with him, beside his own personal workouts. It seems like everything that Itzler is doing is like warm-up exercises to SEAL. This is not surprising, as the man is known order himself to do push-ups. He does it anywhere, anytime, and in front of anyone.

Today, they achieved a six-mile run, a fifteen-minute treadmill test, fifty box jumps, thirty-six pull-ups, and a hundred push-ups.

# Chapter 5: Escape Vehicle

Today, SEAL brings an inflatable raft with four oars to Itzler. He says that it is a means of escape for a national emergency, wherein almost everything shuts down. He means it as an escape pod for the Itzler family. Sara is not so bright with the idea—mainly because it seems a bit unrealistic. Nevertheless, in the end, they agreed that it could be handy.

Hours later, SEAL introduces him to a new routine. He calls it the "one hundred workout". That is what he calls it, but it is actually a "five hundred workout". The reason behind that is because they did a hundred bench presses, repeated twice with no rest, and thirty-pound weighs but end with twenty-pounders. The total would be 200. Next, they did a hundred lateral pull-downs, which they repeated two times, and a hundred shoulder presses. That would be 300. Added up, that would make it "five hundred workout".

The day does not end there. SEAL made a friend at the gym who let him borrow his fifty-pound weight vest. SEAL makes Itzler put it on and do fifteen sets of ten push-ups. This was an extremely difficult exercise for Itzler, because SEAL found it quite difficult.

Today, they did the five hundred workout.

## Señoras de la Limieza

SEAL's being in the apartment is attracting quite the attention. Sara's friends are visiting more often for no apparent reason. The Spanish housekeepers seem to be spending extra time in the work when it came to the Itzler's apartment. They go into SEAL's room even though he is in there. SEAL does not give any of these women even a bit of his attention. He shows no sign of interest as he already has a wife. He sees them as a menace to his privacy. A "security breach" if you may.

Discipline is SEAL's life. He wishes to spread this necessity into everyone's life—including the staff of the fancy apartment. He feels it is his duty. It may be. He suggests that the staff who are not exerting their above-maximum effort on their jobs, be relieved of duty. This seems only fair.

# Chapter 6: That Damn Finger

Itzler awoke at 4 am by the sounds of frustrated noises. He forces himself to get out of bed to investigate. He goes into the living room and finds SEAL on the couch, getting upset he could not get the television to turn on. He continues to let out his rage on the remote. At the same time, he is silently cursing at the complex device. Itzler calmly takes the remote from SEAL and turns on the television for him, and then returns the remote to him. This action causes SEAL to calm down. After solving the noise problem, Itzler went back to bed.

Two hours later, the door opening little by little awakens Itzler. He could feel the presence of someone entering the room. Then he feels a finger touching his shoulder. It did not look like it was Sara's, so he dismissed this as a trick-of-the-mind. After feeling the same finger a couple of times, Itzler heard SEAL's deep voice telling him to get out of bed. He realized it was not his imagination, so he springs up in alarm. Sara, who is sleeping right next to him, does not get affected one bit.

SEAL explained that they would run six miles this morning and that it would be the last of the basic training. He said that the real training would start soon. They head to Central Park, which is Itzler's favourite place to train. Since it was early in the morning, there were only a few vehicles on the road, which made SEAL a bit unhappy, as it was not much of a challenge without an obstacle course.

That day, SEAL decided to step it up by increasing their running speed. When Itzler got home, he was soaked in his sweat even though it was cold and windy outside. Itzler is tired, but he follows one rule that allows him to have the energy to get him through the day; fruit until noon. This was some health advice his friend, Harvey Diamond had given him. It was very effective.

Now Itzler has to go to work. SEAL decides to join him in his office. While Itzler worked on his computer, SEAL just sits in a chair—just being SEAL. It seems like he is thinking hard about something. Suddenly, he stands up and orders Itzler to do burpees. Itzler, who is still in his presentable work outfit, immediately gets down and tries to move at a satisfying pace. He decides to take off his clothes, leaving him in his boxers. A co-worker, Jennifer Kish walks in on the action that was taking place. She immediately turns away without saying a word or taking a second glance and shuts the door. Itzler has no choice but to keep going.

Itzler completes his task and gets back into his work outfit, returning to his previous task.

SEAL had been with Itzler the whole day. They even walked home together. When they got home, SEAL asked Itzler about his interest in Knicks. It was a small question, but it started a friendly conversation between the two. This is a big thing, as SEAL is involved in the little chat. It was surprising that SEAL tried to engage in little debate with Itzler. It revealed a good deal of how SEAL would act around the people he was comfortable with. It is true that people who make an effort to keep a conversation going whether it be a debate or a casual chat, care about the person or are developing feelings for the person.

The conversation let Itzler remember the time when he was younger and had dreams to make a hit song. All he ever wanted was to obtain a record deal and get to be on MTV. He was a young-adult recording artist. This was one of those big dreams that youth enables us to have. Although Jesse Itzler did not become one of those big stars, he did get a chance. There was a time where one of his creations became catchy. To him, this is a big accomplishment. That was a success for him.

SEAL suggests that they continue the chat outdoors while

performing some workout exercises. Itzler agrees. This is an opportunity for him to get to know SEAL better and gives them a higher chance of becoming good friends.

Today, they did twelve miles with six miles escalation pace, three hundred push-ups, and one hundred burpees.

# Chapter 7: Mix Up Your Runs

SEAL feels that Itzler should be training his legs more. He makes Itzler run as fast as he can for long periods. It would seem that Itzler has grown more comfortable with SEAL. Comfortable enough that he let out a small complaint about his legs aching. SEAL, returned the favour by not looking at him coldly. He was satisfied to know that Itzler was improving the way he wanted him to. To express his satisfaction, he made Itzler do two hundred seventy-five push-ups when they arrived home.

SEAL seemed to have opened up a little about his life. He mentioned to Itzler that he was a wannabe-Rambo when he was a child. Perhaps even until now. He said that this is what motivated him to train. He wanted to join the Special Forces.

This is the part where Itzler realizes that he could be making a terrible mistake. It was only now that he realized how vulnerable he and his family was to SEAL. At any moment, he could get rid of them, without a trace. This idea was certainly tempting to believe, but there was also the fact that SEAL is doing things to protect the family. He is clearly acting like a guard dog.

They show up at the headquarters of Spanx, Sara's company that was located in Atlanta. Spanx is a company that Sara started herself. They were having a house built near that area because of the fact that they visit often.

Itzler started to remember the time when he and his partner, Kenny Dichter had started "Marquis Jet". It was some convenient way for people who often fly in jets.

SEAL later on saves Itzler and a woman from a giant branch struck by lightning. This may have convinced Itzler that SEAL was definitely a man whom you can trust with your life. His doubts soon faded away.

Today, they ran seventeen miles and did two hundred seventy-five push-ups earlier that morning.

# Chapter 8: No Peeing Allowed

They leave Atlanta and fly back to Teterboro airport. SEAL and Itzler prepare to go out running. Itzler is not feeling very well—probably dehydrated. He drinks two glasses of water before taking off. Because of this, Itzler has to urinate a short while after they started. He attempts to ask SEAL for permission to stop, but SEAL is not very happy with this. Itzler decides to keep going. When they were finished, SEAL gave him his permission.

During breakfast—an hour later, Itzler noticed that SEAL had not eaten anything ever since he arrived a week ago. Unable to hold her curiosity any longer, Sara asked SEAL about his diet. This led to him explaining to Sara about his whole reasoning for life. Itzler noticed that SEAL did not seem too comfortable with answering all of Sara's innocent questions, so he changed the subject by suggesting a Christmas holiday at the lake house in Connecticut. SEAL agreed, saying that he would gladly check their security in the area. Itzler lets him do so and asks his driver, Smith to drive him.

Itzler met Darnell Smith during his music career. He was a friend of Jay Master Jay of Run-DMC. He was in his office often and Jay ended up giving Smith a job.

Smith and SEAL get to the house in Connecticut. Before bedtime, Itzler asks for a report from Smith. Everything seemed to be all right. Maybe everything would have stayed all right if Smith had not snuck downstairs for a midnight snack and set off the motion sensor alarm by accident. Smith thought it would be the end of him if SEAL were to mistake him for an intruder, so he was literally crying for his life.

SEAL brings up security being flawed based on his survey. He goes on suggesting to Itzler what he should do to make the house bulletproof. This is something that SEAL was taking seriously, so Itzler brought it up with Sara. Sara is not very enthusiastic about spending almost a million dollars for "possible" insane security breaches—that may never happen.

Today, they ran a total of six miles.

# Google Me, Motherfucker

It turns out that SEAL was the one who cracked the tile in the bathroom of the house in Connecticut. He did this to scare away the plumber—a "do not come back" effort. This obviously infuriated the plumber, but SEAL also intimidated him. The plumber is pitiful, as he just wants to make a living.

SEAL will always be "this" protective of his friends. He acts as soon as he suspects.

# Chapter 9: Oxygen Deprivation

Today, Itzler wakes up like a mannequin—stiff. He is not really feeling pain, but he cannot move his body properly. Just reaching out for something is difficult. He tries to tell SEAL that it may be due to the lack of stretching or warm-up exercises. Naturally, SEAL gets offended and gives him that cold stare.

They start with running and find a tree with a long sturdy-looking branch. SEAL tells Itzler to do ten pull-ups. After that, they return home and Itzler takes a hot bath before preparing for a meeting in his conference room later that day.

The meeting is about a new business idea. SEAL sat in the conference room without saying a word while the meeting went on. Itzler could sense something was bothering SEAL. The team decides to take a short break. SEAL tells Itzler about his problem. He said that his mind was nagging him to complete the "unfinished" training from this morning. He tells Itzler to get down and do sit-ups. When that was out of the way, the meeting resumed.

Later that night, a strange, loud noise was coming from

SEAL's room. Itzler goes upstairs to check. SEAL does not answer immediately, but yells after the last few times. Inside the room, there was a camping tent set up. There was some sort of generator with a hose connected to the tent. SEAL explains that he will trap himself inside the tent ad that the generators will suck up all the oxygen inside. This was SEAL's method of training himself.

Today, they went six miles, did ten pull-ups, and did a hundred sit-ups.

# Chapter 10: The Honor Code

This is the point where Jesse Itzler may be regretting his decision of asking SEAL to teach him his ways. He looks back at everything that happened ever since SEAL came into his life. It did not look pretty. It was only at this time that Itzler realized that a normal person would have reacted differently from him in his situation. A normal person would have gone mad. A normal person would have just given up and sent SEAL on his way. A normal person would have been a quitter. At some point, he wanted to stop. It did not sound very nice, but Itzler did not care much at that point. All he knew was that he was tired.

Itzler remembered how much he looked up to SEAL –how he still looks up to SEAL. He remembered that he wanted to become just like him. In conclusion, he could start by honoring the condition that SEAL asked of him.
He immediately got out of bed and got ready for the workout.

After their workout routine, SEAL tells Itzler that he needs to be gone for three days. SEAL orders that he stick to the program while he is away. He told him to do everything on the honor code.

Itzler gives SEAL his word. He cannot help but feel curious as to why he might be leaving.

Today, they did a two-mile interval run, did one hundred seventy-one push-ups, and thirty pull-ups.

## Date Night?

Since SEAL would be absent for three days, Sara decides that this is an opportunity for her and Jesse to "catch up" on each other. Jesse owes her this for her compliance to letting SEAL stay in their home. With SEAL always in the house, it was not very comfortable for Sara to spend "alone time" with her husband. She liked SEAL, but she still considers him a stranger in these circumstances. This date night is very exciting for the two of them, especially Sara.

Just when they were going to begin, Jesse randomly felt the urge to gobble up his food before even making it to the dinner table. He did not even realize it at first until Sara gave him a concerned look. Even though Sara had to eat alone and Jesse had to watch her eat, their date night was perfect because they were still in-love with each other.

# Three Years Earlier: First Date

Jesse Itzler met Sara at a poker tournament hosted by NetJets, the partner of Marquis Jet. He found out about her because she was one of his customers. Jesse's sales representative sent a photo of her as a suggestion to invite her to the tournament. Sara was one of the handpicked forty to participate. Jesse picked her because she looked cute. The night of the event, Sara was in his group of companions. She did not hang out with them for long because she said it was past her bedtime and that she must turn-in. Jesse Itzler thought this was weird for anyone to do that. However, that is what made her interesting in his eyes. That is how he met the love of his life.

He met her again when she hosted a charity event called the Give a Damn Party, to raise enough money for college scholarships for African women who cannot afford it. The main reason why he was there was to see Sara Blakely. By chance, he obtained information about Sara breaking up with her boyfriend. Jesse took the opportunity to connect with her. He asked her to come with him to the Final Four basketball championship, which happened to be in Atlanta. A few weeks later, he officially started to date her. They went to a spa and a sushi restaurant. Even though some things did not go quite as Sara planned, they had the perfect date. They were in-love with each other.

# Chapters 11-12: Enjoy the Pain

## (not counting the days I was on my own)

For the past few days, Itzler was training by himself and he stuck to the program. He definitely was a man of his word. Sometimes, he thought of SEAL. He felt quite lonely when he did everything alone. He is starting to think that he may be missing the tough man.

Later that day, he received a call from SEAL, telling him that he was on his way back to New York City. He also told him some news. The news was that he finished the tough seventy-five-mile race. He added that he broke all the bones in his feet. SEAL told Itzler that he would not see a doctor as it would be a waste of time.

Late at night, SEAL arrives. Walking seems to be very difficult for him. His feet do not look very pretty. Despite this, he said that he is enjoying it. He said that he wants to savor every bit of the pain. He will not let training be delayed, either.

The next day, Marc Rampolla, the CEO of Zico gives Jesse Itzler a call. He asked if SEAL would endorse Zico, stating that it would be a good idea. Itzler is reluctant, but he decides to stay open-minded. He said it is a good idea to ask him.

Itzler did not have much luck with that matter. SEAL immediately rejected any involvement Itzler was trying to introduce to him. Itzler decided not to push.

Later in the afternoon, Itzler hears loud music coming from SEAL's room. It was the theme from the movie "Rocky" and it was on repeat. Itzler decides to stay outside of SEAL's room to listen. When SEAL walks out, he looks like he poured a bucket of water over his head. No, he may have come out of the ocean because of the wet, salty smell. According to him, he did two thousand five hundred push-ups. Sara also checks to see what is happening. I did not know why, but she started to become pale—as if she was seeing a ghost. However, she was not looking at SEAL. When Itzler realized what was bothering Sara, it was too late. His eyes travelled downward and caught sight of Sara's family rug. A puddle in the middle of the rug that her grandmother gave her. Sara spoke to Jesse Itzler in the coldest tone. The tone was scarier than his mother's cold shoulder and death glare.

In a few minutes, SEAL and Itzler head down to the gym, to

give him some hardcore training.

Today, Itzler did a five-minute walk on a steep incline, ran eight miles with two miles intervals, one hundred thirty-two sit-ups, and four hundred eighty-four push-ups.

# Chapter 13: Sick Fuck Friday

Itzler slept less than eight hours last night. That does not sound good since he did four hundred eighty-four push-ups last night, before he went to bed. As usual, SEAL is awake and full of energy. He had been observing the outdoors for their training path. Everybody looks gloomy. SEAL says that today is not all right.

Despite the fact that he is still limping, SEAL runs five miles at a fast pace. SEAL has even been going for challenging paths, like hills. They must maintain that fast pace whichever path they set foot on. For Itzler, going uphill was the most difficult part. His shoulders hurt on every posture and angle he tries. His arms are dangling like that of a ragdoll. Very soon, his whole body may end up the same.

Because Itzler felt excruciatingly weak, he decided to work from home for this day. He spent his work session making calls. Even this task was difficult for him to do. He could barely lift his cell phone. His biceps were numb. To make matters worse, SEAL told him that he was to do more push-ups that night.

SEAL left for the gym and came back two hours later. He held up his hands, exposing his fried-skinned palm. He said that he had done six hundred pull-ups in two hours. He said that all you have to do is think about someone else who is suffering very badly, and exert as much pain to your body as you can, to get even with that person.

SEAL does not come out of his room for hours. Itzler concluded that he is sleeping. He takes the opportunity to do the same thing. Without changing into sleeping clothes, he lays back and drifts off into dreamland. He is suddenly awoken by his alarm clock in the middle of the night. Itzler realizes that SEAL had set the alarm and it sitting on a chair a few feet away from the bed. Naturally, this was creepy and at the same time nerve-wrecking. He tries to go back to sleep, but SEAL keeps him up. Finally, Itzler springs up.

They trained in the empty, soulless Central Park in the dark. It was an hour past midnight—what could anyone expect? To make matters worse, it was a winter midnight. As soon as they got back, Itzler threw on a winter jacket and went to sleep next to Sara.

Today, they ran eight miles, did eight hundred jumping jacks, and did two hundred push-ups.

# Lady in the Honda

SEAL and Itzler are on their way to the house in Connecticut to check some things. When they arrived, the made sure everything was in place and made their way back to New York. On the way back, SEAL is driving and Jesse is giving him directions. SEAL starts doing a driving technique that he used in the military. To point out "potential threats". He started pointing at a woman driving a Honda with her kids at the back. He said that she could also be a threat in some way. It is not a good idea to look away, even for a split-second.

# Chapter 14: Fireman's Carry

SEAL decides to do something new with Jesse Itzler today. He introduces something called "fireman carries". According to SEAL it is basic military training. Some difficulties Itzler had to deal with were the rush and the awkwardness of the situation. He did not enjoy carrying SEAL and he most certainly did not enjoy being carried by the man. He was rough with him and just carried and threw him around like a ragdoll. They were doing this on a residential elevator. Their neighbors found the situation freaky yet extraordinary. One even commented that it "looks a bit intense". For Itzler, this was insanity.

Later in the afternoon, Itzler finds SEAL in his office talking to someone on the phone. He says that it is Kevin Garnett on the other line. Itzler found it nice that they were keeping in touch with each other. Then, SEAL hangs up and orders Itzler to do burpees. He does a hundred and feels good about himself.

Just when Jesse Itzler was about to slump into bed coming home from a late night New York Knicks game, he heard a familiar voice tell him to run eight miles. He tries to sound pitiful and begs that they do it early the next morning instead. SEAL gave him something called "the Look", which seemed to be enough to drive Itzler to do what he wanted him to do.

Today, they ran six miles, did fourteen "fireman carries", and Itzler did a hundred burpees.

# Chapter 15: It's All About the Push-ups

Itzler goes into the kitchen. He sees SEAL with his "thinking face" on again. SEAL announces that they should step up their training. He says that they do six miles plus two AFAWC (As Fast as We Can). Itzler tries to dress up like SEAL. Why not? It is around twenty-eight degrees outdoors. Itzler feels that he is more comfortable in this light outfit. During the run, SEAL is using his superhuman senses again instead of his watch.

Itzler feels amazingly good. He can actually feel himself improving. He pats himself on the back for doing an amazing job.

They go to LaGuardia for a flight to Atlanta. It is a matter of business for Sara at her company. Instead of Marquis Jet, they use Delta. SEAL does not really mind. He will go anywhere as long as he knows firsthand. He does not like last-minute plans. Normally, SEAL will do push-ups ANYWHERE.

SEAL seems to be talkative today. He wants to know more about Jesse Itzler. It does not matter to him what kind of information Itzler gives him—he just wants to know something about him. Itzler tells him more about his short-term music career. He said that he wanted to start his own record label, even though he was freeloading in his friends' homes. He did not always have a guaranteed pay, because not everything sold. There were many bumps in the way. One of those bumps was a girl named Crystal. He thought that they would get big through her—but she actually ruined everything. Up to this day, Itzler still ponders how that night ended up in shambles. He lost the money he had earned from his own album to Riot Records, because of Crystal.

As soon as they land, his friend, Lisa, greets Itzler. She happened to be on the same flight. None of them had noticed until they landed. Itzler introduces her to SEAL.

A few hours later, they arrived at the house in Atlanta. SEAL orders Itzler to do proper push-ups. By the time they were finished, it was around midnight.

Today, they ran eight miles with two miles of AFAWC and three hundred fifty proper push-ups.

# Perfect Position

SEAL and the Itzler family are having dinner at a restaurant called 10 Degrees South, owned by one of their friends. Even during this time, SEAL has his back against the wall, observing everything he can get his senses on. He declares that he is in a perfect position. SEAL is jumpy to every little sound. He gets suspicious of the waiter that is serving them. He says that the waiter seems to be very—off.

Jesse and Sara start to believe him. They keep a close eye at the waiter.

# Chapter 16: Stay Lite

The next day, Sara goes to headquarters to manage things. SEAL and Jesse go out for a run three miles down the main road, Peachtree. There are several different Peachtree roads, but it does not really matter to them which one they take. The streets are congested with some slow-moving traffic. They are running near the cars that are on halt at red traffic lights. The two runners get the attention of drivers as they run past. SEAL was especially getting that attention. It gets so much attention that even Sara knows their location due to her co-workers talking about how they saw SEAL running on the street, on their way to work.

They catch a flight and arrive at around two-thirty in the afternoon. SEAL received a delivery. The delivery was something he ordered for Jesse. It is a metal-plated weight vest for push-ups and challenged runs. It increases the brutality of the training. It looks like a suicide bomber's vest. SEAL is enjoying the vest. They ran for an hour and Jesse falls asleep on the couch when they got home, exhausted.

An hour later, SEAL orders Jesse to grab the vest and go outdoors to run. Jesse says that he cannot leave Lazer in the house. As a result, SEAL tells him to bring the toddler with them. They take turns using the vest while running and pushing the stroller. Everyone who say them were disgraced because they had a toddler out in the cold, for a workout. Jesse just shakes it off and SEAL does not care.

Jesse orders some food when they got back home. He offers SEAL some food, but he declines saying that he needs to go "light". SEAL dismisses himself to his room with a banana and some almonds.

Today, they ran seventeen mile with five point five miles in a fifty-pound vest.

# Chapter 17: Suicide Bombers

SEAL and Jesse are in the gym. SEAL is preparing the equipment for their routine. As soon as he is satisfied with the arrangement, SEAL explains the routine. While they do some bench presses, a resident and friend of Jesse, Bob Costas, is attentively watching the two men. Today, SEAL gives Jesse his first compliment. He said he did nice work.

SEAL decides to tag along with Jesse to work. They walk every morning to the office—wearing weight vests under their shirts. Jesse is not very keen on the idea of having to walk on the streets looking like a terrorist, but he liked walking with SEAL. They have become closer since the first time they met. SEAL asks Jesse questions about what to do with the money he saved from his time in the military. Jesse gives him advice that Sara had given him regarding money. SEAL liked Sara's advice. It put a smile on his face whenever Jesse cited one of Sara's quotations.

SEAL has softened up a lot ever since their first meeting, but he is still very sharp. He is still suspicious of the little details that seem to be "off"—which is a good thing. One time he insisted that they take a longer route to the office to avoid Trump Tower. He said that it might be dangerous as Trump is getting a lot of attention these days.

At two in the afternoon, the go to the gym to do a second workout for the day. During the workout on the treadmill, Jesse lets out a fart and starts to laugh hysterically when SEAL mimics the sound effect. SEAL does not laugh or even grin.

After the workout, Jesse wants to go to Barneys to buy gifts for Sara and Lazer. Obviously, SEAL is coming with him. He insists that they run to and from the store. Jesse brings nothing but his credit card and some emergency cash—for emergencies.

They go to the jewelry section first. SEAL keeps commenting on how pointless it was to spend money on jewelry. Jesse says that he wants to get a gift for the sake of giving one, this holiday. He buys some items and have them wrapped. They run back home carrying the shopping bags from Barneys.

Today, Jesse ran three miles or twenty-five minutes of intervals on treadmill, did four hundred sixty-five push-ups, fifty sit-ups, fifty flutter kicks, and did SEAL circuit that consists of dumbbell bench presses, seated rows, military press, tri pull-downs, and curls.

# Chapter 18: The Difference Five Minutes Can Make

Jesse gets the day off. The first thing he does in the morning is play with Lazer. He spends his time with his son. Later that day, SEAL went in to remind Jesse that he has an afternoon meeting with the Zico sales team. He must part with his son for a moment. They get ready to walk to the office. SEAL seems to be feeling chilly. He is wearing a shirt and a pair of jeans. They did not wear the weight vests today because Sara convinced SEAL that it was not a very good idea. They are taking a straight route to the office. They are commuting normally, as normal buddies would do.

They had a conversation about how Jesse handles his life. Jesse tells SEAL that the best thing to do in a bad situation is to try to control that situation. SEAL is impressed by his way of life.

When Jesse began his work, he decided to ask SEAL if he could leave the room, just for that time. SEAL took a chair and sat outside, as if he was guarding the door. He probably was. Jesses relaxes on his chair, reminiscing the past. He was so relaxed that he fell asleep drooling on his desk. A few hours later, SEAL walks in and suggests that they get out of the office. It was evening when SEAL and Jesse bumped into Yoni at the gym. Yoni is Jesse's twenty-four-year-old nephew. SEAL insisted that Yoni join them in their workout.

Yoni and SEAL step out to workout. Jesse stayed in the apartment to wait for them. SEAL recommended that Yoni join the Navy and become a Navy SEAL like him. The workout would be to test if he has a chance to succeed. After nearly two hours, SEAL got back to the apartment, Yoni nowhere to be found. A few more hours passed, Yoni walks through the door of the apartment. He does not look too good—like he could pass out any minute now. He declared that he was not fit for the training the Navy was going to offer him.

Today, Jesse did three hundred sixty-four push-ups, thirty pull-ups, and a hundred flutter kicks.

# Chapter 19: My Shoulders

Today, they started their usual routine at their usual time. Jesse wishes he could just stay in bed and watch the morning program with Sara. But he remembers that SEAL will be here until next week. He does not want to disappoint SEAL. Not after forming a bond he wished to have with the man. He gets up.

Jesse has a meeting with the team of a big hotel chain. As usual, SEAL follows him and insists that they were the weight vests to the meeting. As usual, SEAL becomes the center of attention in the conference room. Although they did not talk much about the actual topic they were supposed to be discussing, Jesse was satisfied that the team wanted to have something to do with him—even if they really after SEAL and his stories.

Later that night, Jesse has a holiday party with his business team and SEAL comes along. Jesse is dumbfounded by SEAL's unusual attack on the food that was served there. SEAL ate EVERTHING but dessert. He consumed more than half of the food that was served at the party. Like always, he was showered with questions from the staff. They all took the opportunity interview SEAL tonight because he does not say a word to them whenever it is a usual day at the office. All in all, they both enjoyed the little celebration.

As if he was a machine programmed to do things it does not want to do, Jesse got ready for a workout as soon as they got home. It was difficult for him to do push-ups while drunk and at the same time, beat.

Today, they ran six miles at a sub-8-minute-mile pace and two hundred push-ups.

# Chapter 20: Start When the Second Hand Hits

It is pretty gloomy this morning. Jesse looks out the window—not a soul on the street. SEAL announces that they will be doing basic exercises today. They are just as important as all the brutal "soul-heart-muscle" training that Jesse had to go through. Jesse definitely gets tired of the exercises that they had to do for hours. However, he is looking much better than he looked the first time he trained with SEAL. He is doing a better job.

Jesse's days of brutality pay-off when he is visited by his friend, Bryan Fried. SEAL suggests that Fried join Jesse in his workout. Bryan Fried is in good shape, but he is unable to keep up with Jesse. They finish the little workout with Jesse looking better than Bryan. SEAL shows that he is proud of him.

Jesse and SEAL go for a little "cooldown" outdoors. There was not a single soul during the run other than one other runner and a dog barking in the distance.

A few minutes later, they need to get to the airport and fly to

Atlanta. Sara apparently has a meeting tomorrow morning. Jesse and Seal come with her so she would not feel lonely. Although Jesse would rather stay home and work, SEAL says it is best to come with her. They leave in the middle of the night.

Today, they ran eight miles, did four hundred push-ups, and did five hundred fifty sit-ups.

## White Van

The very next day, Jesse finds SEAL looking out the window, watching the street like a hawk. He is on alert for a white van that he said was stalking them. He is dead serious—the white van "breached" their security. He spotted that white van the previous night when he was on a security watch. He did not get to read the plate number, but he assures Jesse that he obtain this information—perhaps even more. He assures Jesse that he be looking out for those who dare to breach the safety of the Itzlers.

# Chapter 21: One Rep at a Time

They are back in New York City as soon as Sara had taken care of her business. SEAL and Jesse go run in the park. Jesse is thinking of how grateful he is to have SEAL in his life.

They go home and eat a light meal. Immediately after eating, SEAL wants them to go out on another run. Jesse is thinking this is a bad idea, but they do it anyway. The sicker Jesse got, the faster the running pace got.

Today, they ran ten miles at an eight-minute mile pace.

# Chapters 22-23: Night Training

It is Christmas in New York City. The streets are lit up beautifully. Most are indoors, celebrating the holiday instead of being out on the street. The Itzlers, along with SEAL decide to celebrate at the house in Connecticut. Jesse and SEAL head out for a quick run before they have the traditional gift-opening ceremony of the holiday.

SEAL gives a gift to Lazer, saying that he has the potential to be a soldier. The gift is a tiny soldier uniform—not a costume. Next, Sara hands SEAL a gift from the Itzler family. He is given a dress shirt. He attempts to politely refuse to try it on in front of the Itzler family. He gave in to Sara's request to wear it because she practically ordered him to. It looked good on him; however he did not seem comfortable. He was not used to it. Then, Jesse gave Sara the present he bought from Barneys. She liked the necklace and appreciated Jesse's effort to get her the little gift.

SEAL is playing with Lazer and his toys. They were doing a realistic role-play of a raid and Lazer enjoyed it. SEAL did not really take it as "just a role-play". The adults have a movie night as soon as Lazer goes to sleep.

SEAL wakes Jesse at two in the morning for a run in the mountains. Jesse silently gets ready as to not wake Sara. They are running on a snowy mountain and it is pitch-black—SEAL can see perfectly well in the dark. To make matters worse for Jesse, snow is falling like arrows from the sky. When they finished, Jesse put all his clothes in the dryer and went to bed.

They go for another run a few hours later. They finish and wait for a few more hours before running again. Then SEAL promised that this would be their last run for the day, which is definitely good news for Jesse. This was convenient because Jesse injured himself during the run and cannot continue running. SEAL tells him to do push-ups for compensation.

He mentioned Grant Hill—someone from his past. He and Kenny were hired to do a national radio campaign. It was some competition and they won because he completed a task—to get the NBA's Rookie of the Year, Grant Hill, in their commercial. Jesse tells SEAL the whole story. SEAL says it is a funny story; however he might have been being sarcastic.

Jesse almost did a thousand push-ups—but that was as far as

he could go. SEAL begs him to keep going; however it is impossible at the moment. They call it a day.

Today, they ran sixteen point one miles and Jesse did seven hundred push-ups.

# Chapter 24: Whiteout

There was a blizzard the next morning. Unsurprisingly, SEAL insists that they go for a run—he cannot stay still, even after hearing the announcement that the outdoors are extremely unsafe. He even wears the fifty-pound weight vest for the whole run.

After lunch, Sara goes out to get the mail. SEAL is disturbed by this, saying that she does the same thing at the same time. He says she is predictable. Predictable is bad in SEAL's book.

They have dinner and get into bed. A few hours later, Jesse finds Sara still awake ad trying to quietly get out of bed. She says that she hears something in the basement and is going to investigate. It was the sound of the generator turned on. Sara gets back into bed and says that it is nothing.

The noise continued the whole night—even in the morning. Jesse goes down to the basement to look. He finds SEAL using the stationary bike. He had been going the whole night.

Today, they ran three point five miles and did one hundred fifty four push-ups.

# Chapter 25: Get Your Balls Wet

After going on their morning run, Jesse's foot is swollen and painful. SEAL suggests that they jump into the cold lake to numb the pain. When they get there, SEAL jumps right in and orders Jesse to jump in. When Jesse got it, SEAL suddenly tells him to get out. He says that they have five minutes before frostbite. Jesse panics. They must run up a steep hill to get back to the house. When they reach the house, they warm themselves up with everything they can find. Sara is infuriated when she sees them. She scolds Jesse, and then turns to SEAL. He defends himself by saying that this is what Jesse signed up for.

A few minutes later, they do push-ups. Jesse is thinking that this whole day is insane, yet he is proud of himself.

Later, SEAL walks into Jesse's bedroom where Jesse is trying to numb the swollen ankle. SEAL tells Jesse that they only have a few days left and that they need to step-up their game. He tells Jesse that they will go into the steam room—to test Jesse's willpower. Before they go in, SEAL sets the temperature insanely high. It is above boiling point. They have to sit up straight in there, for thirty minutes. When Jesse was around seventy-five percent of the way, he breaks. He runs out of the room and stays against the wall. SEAL feels sorry for him, so he "aborts" the test.

A few hours later, SEAL tells Jesse to jog outdoors by himself. When Jesse comes back, he is ordered to do a hundred push-ups or else he cannot go inside.

While Jesse is preparing his dinner, SEAL gives him a choice to do push-ups after eating or do something else before eating. Jesse chose option number two and did push-ups and sit-ups.

Today, Jesse ran nine point five miles, did seven hundred seventy-five sit-ups, one hundred twenty-five sit-ups, twenty-one-minutes in the steam room, and a near-frostbite experience.

# Chapter 26: Primary Target

Jesse feels better from yesterday's incident. They go for a run and Jesse relaxes when they finished.

Jesse and SEAL get into some "real talk". Jesse asked SEAL what he would do if the family's safety is in danger. SEAL answered what everyone knows he would answer; protect the family. Although SEAL cares about Jesse, Sara and Lazer occupy the softest part in SEAL's heart and they would be his first priority if something bad were to happen.

Jesse spends a few hours on his work without SEAL distracting him. Then they go out for a run.

Today, they ran nine point five miles.

# Chapter 27: 1,000 Push-ups

SEAL decides that today is the day that Jesse will do a thousand push-ups. Jesse does as many push-ups as he can every few hours. Later in the afternoon, he had accomplished a thousand push-ups. They go for a run after a few hours. SEAL gives Jesse a small compliment by telling him to sleep well and that he earned it. SEAL heads up to his room and does his own push-ups—two thousand five hundred of them. Jesse has never been so proud of himself.

Today, they ran three point five miles and achieved a thousand push-ups.

# Chapter 28: Up the Ante

In the morning, they go for a run on a complex course. Jesse manages this and has fun. Then SEAL suggests that they go back to the lake. This time, the lake is frozen solid. SEAL tells Jesse that he has a plan for this. Sara is not so happy with the idea, yet the two sneak out of the house when she was not looking. SEAL smashes the solid ice with a boulder. He is very happy with his accomplishment and jumps into the ice. They repeat jumping into the ice and run home fast. Jesse feels so much better than he did last time. Sara is waiting by the door with Lazer. She looks like a mom glaring at her two kids. Even SEAL is intimidated and cannot look at her. Half of the day, Sara gave them the "cold shoulder". She did not stay mad for long.

Jesse and Sara are packing for Atlanta later that night. They start to talk about SEAL and how they are going to miss him when he is gone. Sara liked having SEAL around them. She told Jesse that she would like to ask SEAL if he would train her too. Jesse thinks this is a good idea.

Today, they ran eight point five miles, did three hundred push-ups, and jumped in the frozen lake—twice.

# Chapter 29: Sloppy Seconds

Before they left for Atlanta to check-up on the progress of the house construction, SEAL and Jesse go out for a run. They take a difficult course to a diner. The course was so difficult and SEAL was so impatient that Jesse got there—twenty minutes after SEAL. Sara picks them up from the diner, in a car.

A few more hours later, SEAL is making Jesse do more workouts, saying that they must maximize it before they leave for the airport. They had to skip the last set because Sara would be furious if they were late.

Today, they ran ten point six miles, twenty minutes on the treadmill inclined at fifteen, did one hundred push-ups, and did thirty pull-ups.

# The Skinheads

The Itzlers are in Atlanta. Jesse is alone in the backyard, reading. Their cleaning lady alerts him that there are two men outside, looking for the owner of the house. They do not look very friendly.

Jesse goes out to meet them. He tells them that he is only a guest and not the owner. They do not seem to be living around there. Jesse found it obvious that they were lying about being new to the neighborhood because they told him that they met up with Usher—saying that he lived in this neighborhood, which was a false fact. They are acting intimidating—telling him to get the owner of the house to meet them. Jesse has had enough, so he goes inside and alerts SEAL. A little later, SEAL comes back with picture in his phone of one of the men. He was jacked up. SEAL assures Jesse that the bullies will never come back to this house—or any other house in the neighborhood, if you may.

# Resolutions

New Year's Eve has come. The Itzlers celebrate it by inviting their closest friends to the lake house. They plan to have a little "show and tell" of their New Year's resolutions. While having dinner, they start the conversation about resolutions. Of course, everyone is curious about what SEAL has to say for himself. He tells everyone that he is not going to resolve for anything. He politely gets off the table and goes to the basement to use the stationary bike. He must have felt guilty for being a little harsh during dinner, so he comes back up and rephrases his last sentence.

# Chapter 30: Last Run

They drove back to New York City in the afternoon. Jesse and SEAL did not workout in the morning. Sara decides to ask SEAL if he could train her. He tells her that he will be leaving tomorrow for business and that he would come back to train her. SEAL gave the same condition he gave to Jesse—thirty days ago. Today, SEAL is in a good mood. They go out for a run. The routine did not change even though it is their last run together. SEAL is still silently running with Jesse even though it is going to be his last run—as his trainer.

Today, they ran their last six miles together.

# Chapter 31: A Sad Chapter

Today is SEAL's takeoff. He took off—without telling Jesse he was leaving. The only things that told Jesse he had left, is a note and a one hundred percent SEAL-free room. Jesse almost cannot believe it is over. That "today" existed.

Even if there is no evidence in the guest room that SEAL was living in the apartment, you can tell he was there because of all the safety equipment that was not there before. A fire extinguisher is planted in every room—along with some fire suits and an inflatable raft, for the whole family.

Jesse Itzler feels like a different person—a better person.

# EPILOGUE

A few months later, Sara and Jesse are going on a vacation to Bahamas. They invited SEAL and he came along. Like the SEAL he always is, he did not come with anything but a bike and a stationary bike. The whole short-stay, SEAL was working out in his room. He was training for a bike marathon across the country.

A year later, SEAL calls Jesse who is working in the office. He tells him that he will be in the city to attend some meetings. Jesse invites him to stay in their apartment, but SEAL declines the offer—saying he will sleep in the park.

# Conclusion

Jesse Itzler wanted to change his life—without changing his life. He wanted to have a better outlook in life—without changing the life, he had already achieved. He was able to achieve his goal because he was fortunate enough to hire someone like "SEAL". Itzler's goal was not an easy one; it is not an easy transition. It involved developing a base—that is already developed. Many sacrifices had to be made, to win. He had to follow every rule that was given to him and do everything he was told to do—without protest. He payed someone to be his boss because he could not be his own boss. Itzler did not know how to transform on his own discipline.

Most people struggle with a sudden transition. They find a problem with change because it breaks their "pattern". They believe that a little change can permanently ruin their lives. Well, this logic is what make this logic true. This logic will surely lead to a life's ruin and discontent. It is a "tragic death". Change is always there. It is hiding in the bushes, waiting to pounce on its prey—the living. Change was hired by life. To most, life, is considered the boss of all living things. This is so, because everything happens "because of life". People think that life will shower them will problems and there is nothing they can do about it. That is why most people fail. They give in to their negativity—their self-doubt. This is sad because those people do not see through the illusion. The illusion of life being the enemy. They think life controls them when bad things happen. They become so lost and scared—they do not know what to do. Only few people see that life—it is just a story. It is a story in a book. It can be rewritten. Words can be replaced. It is only possible because the living—they are the authors. They can rewrite things. They control their hands. Although, there may be a certain extent to erasing mistakes with the provided eraser. That is just as far as "control" can extend.

Whatever a person may feel or think as a result of change, is completely their fault.

Jesse Itzler saw through life's illusion—even though he was well off on his own. That may be the reason as to why he was "well off". All through his life, he believed that only he could manipulate life the way he wanted it to be. That is why he got what he wanted in the end. SEAL must have seen it in him. He must have seen that Itzler was not too far away from his own self.

His wife, Sara, must have had many doubts. In some parts of the story, she was telling her husband that "this may be too much for you" or "there is no purpose in feeling this much pain". It is only natural and good for her to be concerned about someone she loves—but why does she do it? Consciously, she is being concerned for his health. Subconsciously, she is curious. She is asking herself; how does this man do it? Naturally, humans keep to themselves and let others do their own business. Nevertheless, Sara was showing concern for her husband; glaring at him whenever he hurt himself. She could easily mind her own business. After all, what her husband is doing is what he wants to do. But her soul is curious—wanting to know his way of life. She wants to know how he can tolerate so much to get where he wants to be.

Jesse Itzler displayed a very good example of how humans should handle life's problems. Since life is very similar to a book, they have similar problems. When writing a book, you can face the "not knowing what to write" problem or the "I have no pencil or paper" problem. Those problems are very similar to the problems people have when dealing with their emotions. You see, there is always an excuse with people. "I cannot draw because I have no arms" and "I cannot think properly because my brain is damaged", generalizes every problem a human could have. It is all inexcusable.

This story really opens up the mind to great topics.

# Final Thoughts

Hey! Did you enjoy this book? We sincerely hope you thoroughly enjoyed this short read and have gotten immensely valuable insights that will help you in any areas of your life.

Would it be too greedy if we ask for a review from you?

It takes 1 minute to leave 1 review to possibly influence 1 more person's decision to read just 1 book which may change their 1 life. Your 1 minute matters and we value it and thank you so much for giving us your 1 minute. If it sucks, just say it sucks. Period.

# FREE BONUS

## P.S. Is it okay if we overdeliver?

Here at Abbey Beathan Publishing, we believe in overdelivering way beyond our reader's expectations. Is it okay if we overdeliver?

Here's the deal, we're going to give you an extremely valuable cheatsheet of "Accelerated Learning". We've partnered up with Ikigai Publishing to present to you the exclusive bonus of "Accelerated Learning Cheatsheet"

What's the catch? We need to trust you... You see, we want to overdeliver and in order for us to do that, we've to trust our reader to keep this bonus a secret to themselves. Why? Because we don't want people to be getting our exclusive accelerated learning cheatsheet without even buying our books itself. Unethical, right?

Ok. Are you ready?

Simply Visit this link: http://bit.ly/acceleratedcheatsheet

We hope you'll enjoy our free bonuses as much as we've enjoyed preparing it for you!

# Free Bonus #2: Free Book Preview of

# Summary: Give and Take

## The Book at a Glance

All throughout our life, we interact with people who have different reciprocity styles. A person may be a giver, a taker, or a matcher. A taker is someone who is concerned of his own interests. They take more than what they give. A matcher is someone who gives the same amount he or she receives. On the other hand, a giver is someone who is concerned of others' well-being. Givers can be classified as selfless givers or otherish givers. Selfless givers are more likely to be doormats and pushovers because they sacrifice their own interests to help others. They are most likely to fail and end up at the bottom. On the other hand, otherish givers are givers who are concerned of others but are also concerned of his or her own interests. They are most likely to be successful.

Otherish givers are proof that assertiveness is not the only factor to get to the top. They show people that giving can be a factor of success. Furthermore, they prove that we don't need to be selfish to achieve success. Giving provides a lot of benefits. It can build networks which you could get access to new information. It can also build long-lasting relationships.

This book aims to inform the readers how givers rise to the top. The author wants to prove that givers are not pushovers and doormats and they are as competent as takers and matchers.

Moreover, the book shows that takers and matchers can shift to the giver direction through helping in the community they belong in. The book does not only intend to inform the readers how giving can help people achieve success but also to encourage readers to be givers to have a richer purpose, more lasting impact, and more success.

The first five chapters of the book contain the principles of giver success, showing how and why givers become successful. The five chapters also include how givers interact in networking, collaborating, evaluating, and influencing.

The last three chapters of the book discuss the benefits and costs of giving. These chapters emphasize how givers manage to avoid burnout and to avoid being pushovers and doormats. These chapters prove that giving can make you happier and live longer.

Chapter 1: Good Returns describes the three reciprocity styles. The chapter discusses the advantages and disadvantages of each reciprocity styles in various situations. Moreover, the chapter includes how each reciprocity style rise to the top. It emphasizes that givers can be successful, too. Stories of David Hornik and Abraham Lincoln were used as an example of success stories of famous givers.

Chapter 2: The Peacock and the Panda discusses how givers, takers, and matchers build their networks and how important networking is in achieving success. The chapter also includes how to spot a taker disguised as a giver, how social media makes it easier for people to identify a person's reciprocity style, how important are weak ties and dormant ties in rising to the top, and how doing a favor that would only take for five minutes or less for someone can be rewarding.

Chapter 3: The Ripple Effect describes how collaboration can put a person in an advantage. It emphasizes how takers and givers differ in a team. It also explains why most givers are not known and how takers dominate the spotlight. Givers do not thirst on taking credits. They usually give away the credit. Moreover, it emphasizes the importance of being empathetic with people.

Chapter 4: Finding the Diamond in the Rough emphasizes how givers recognize potential in people. It also includes how high expectations from others motivate people to perform better. Moreover, the chapter describes how givers hone a person with an untapped potential and when do givers give up a bad talent.

Chapter 5: The Power of Powerless Communication emphasizes how powerless communication can help givers achieve success. Forms of powerless communication are discussed in this chapter. It also includes how useful powerless communication is in presenting, selling, persuading, and negotiating. Also, it emphasizes the importance of modesty in earning respect and prestige.

Chapter 6: The Art of Motivation Maintenance discusses how givers avoid burnout. The chapter also discusses how selfless givers differ from otherish givers. Furthermore, it discusses how do otherish givers rise to the top and why do selfless givers end up at the bottom. Furthermore, the chapter describes otherish strategies such as chunking and the 100-hour rule of volunteering that you could apply in your work or life.

Chapter 7: Chump Change describes how otherish givers avoid becoming doormats and pushovers and how selfless givers overcome the doormat effect. The chapter includes how otherish strategies such as sincerity screening, generous tit for tat, and advocating for others can help avoid the doormat effect.

Chapter 8: The Scrooge Shift discusses how belonging to a community can tilt people into the giver direction. The chapter describes the principle of optimal distinctiveness, uncommon commonality and reciprocity ring.

Chapter 9: Out of The Shadows emphasizes that givers can be on top and there is no reason to hide giver values. It emphasizes that givers are not weak and naïve unlike what people perceive them to be.

"Actions for Impact" presents a set of practical actions the reader can apply in his or her work or life to live by the principle of giving. It includes strategies and habits of successful givers that the reader can apply.

This book will make you reconsider your perception of success. This book is for everyone, regardless of your reciprocity style. If you are a selfless giver, you may gain insights on how to become otherish and make your way to the top. If you are a matcher, you will be surprised at how you can help others without compromising your own success. If you are a taker, you may be tempted to shift into the giver direction. You'll realize that selfishness will not get you to the top. However, it probably won't work if you give just because you want to succeed.

# Chapter 1

## Good Returns

## The Dangers and Rewards of Giving More Than What You Get

In all courses of life, people can identify themselves as givers or takers. Givers are generous people who prioritize the well-being of others than their own well-being. They give more than what they get in return. On the other hand, takers are competitive and self-focused people. They want to be better than others and take more than what they give. However, some people are matchers. They strike a balance between giving and taking. When they give something, they seek something in return. Nonetheless, you might find yourself shifting from one reciprocity style to another.

Each reciprocity style has its own pros and cons. Studies have found that givers are more likely to be at the bottom of the success ladder. Prioritizing others' success and sacrificing their own becomes a disadvantage to givers. Because givers care and trust too much, they are more likely to be less powerful and dominant. If you think takers or matchers are the ones on top of the success ladder, you are wrong. Surprisingly, it's the givers again.

For deeper understanding, the author used David Hornik's story to illustrate how givers might be at a disadvantage but somehow managed to be successful. Danny Shader's idea was to provide a solution to the problem of Americans who have trouble purchasing online because they don't have a bank account or credit card. Shader thought Hornik would be a great investor for his pitch since Hornik's specialization is on Internet companies. Hornik liked Shader's idea but he gave Shader the option to explore more investors before settling with him. He was hoping Shader would choose him and even gave Shader a list of references to prove his competence and trustworthiness. Unfortunately, Shader chose another investor because he thought Hornik was not a challenging investor.

Shader eventually regretted his decision of letting go of the opportunity to work with Hornik. He invited Hornik to become one of his investors, which Hornik gladly accepted. Shader discovered how competent and dedicated Hornik as an investor. He overlooked Hornik's competence and dedication because he thought Hornik was too giving. From then on, Shader recommended Hornik to other investors. It was a win-win situation for both of them. Hornik might have been at a disadvantage as a giver but he eventually became successful because of the same reason.

Givers and takers have different kind of successes. When a taker succeeds, rivals would try to pull them down. In contrast, when givers succeed, people support them instead of pulling them down. The path to success is smoother when you don't have enemies who are trying to pull you down. Some people think that givers are pushovers in politics. However, some politicians who are givers are successful in the field. An example of which is Abraham Lincoln.

Abraham Lincoln is known as one of the best leaders of the world. He was a leader who puts the well-being of the nation before his own well-being. He aspired to be the Clinton of Illinois despite of him being a farm worker. He lacked credentials to be qualified as a politician but he still grabbed the chance to run as a Senator. Sadly, he lost and put up a business which eventually failed, leaving him with debt. At twenty-five years old, he tried his luck and ran for a seat in the state legislature. Fortunately, he won and served the legislature while earning a degree in law. At age forty-five, he tried his luck once again and ran for a seat in the Senate.

He was the most popular candidate, consistently on top of the poll. He competed with James Shields and Lyman Trumbull who were more qualified than him. Joel Matteson entered the picture and swept off the popularity poll, putting Lincoln at second. Lincoln doubted his ability and decided to withdraw from the race. He asked his supporters to vote for Trumbull instead since he and Trumbull shared the same values. His only aim was to prevent Matteson for winning because he knew Matteson has engaged himself in questionable practices. He didn't want such leader to lead his beloved nation.

Trumbull won a seat in the Senate at the expense of Lincoln. People were worried that Lincoln was not capable of making tough political decisions when he withdrew his candidacy. However, Lincoln did not give up on pursuing his interest to serve the nation. He ran for the Senate again, four years after Trumbull had won. Lincoln's sacrifice had paid off when Trumbull rooted for him when he ran again. As we all know, Lincoln eventually become the President of the United States. He appointed his rivals as his cabinet members because he believed the nation needs leaders who are educated, knowledgeable, and experienced. He did not think of himself when he appointed his rivals. Instead, he put the nation's well-being first before his own by appointing men who are worthy to serve the nation and for its betterment.

People tend to overlook the advantages of being a giver. They think givers would not make it to the top because they are weak and naïve. Seemingly, givers become successful in the long run. Givers can succeed in whatever field they choose. However, givers are hesitant to show their giver tendencies because they are afraid to be judged as naïve and weak. Givers can be excellent influencers, too. They help others succeed which eventually establishes a relationship with others. Givers have unique approaches when interacting with other people in networking, collaborating, evaluating, and influencing. Each of the four domains will be discussed thoroughly in the next chapters.

# SUMMARY:

# LOVE AND RESPECT

## THE LOVE SHE MOST DESIRES, THE RESPECT HE DESPERATELY NEEDS

## ABBEY BEATHAN

**Text Copyright © Abbey Beathan**

All rights reserved. No part of this guide may be reproduced
in any form without permission in writing from the publisher
except in the case of brief quotations embodied in critical
articles or reviews.

## Legal & Disclaimer

Legal & Disclaimer

The information contained in this book is not designed to replace or take the place of any form of medicine or professional medical advice. The information in this book has been provided for educational and entertainment purposes only.

The information contained in this book has been compiled from sources deemed reliable, and it is accurate to the best of the Author's knowledge; however, the Author cannot guarantee its accuracy and validity and cannot be held liable for any errors or omissions. Changes are periodically made to this book. You must consult your doctor or get professional medical advice before using any of the suggested remedies, techniques, or information in this book. Images used in this book are not the same as of that of the actual book. This is a totally separate and different entity from that of the original book titled: "Love and Respect: The Love She Most Desires; The Respect He Desperately Needs."

Upon using the information contained in this book, you agree to hold harmless the Author from and against any damages, costs, and expenses, including any legal fees potentially resulting from the application of any of the information provided by this guide. This disclaimer applies to any damages or injury caused by the use and application, whether directly or indirectly, of any advice or information presented, whether for breach of contract, tort, negligence, personal injury, criminal intent, or under any other cause of action.

You agree to accept all risks of using the information presented inside this book. You need to consult a professional medical practitioner in order to ensure you are both able and healthy enough to participate in this program.

# The Book at a Glance

This book is about how both the husband and the wife can appreciate, respect, and understand each other.

This book has three parts. The first part is about the crazy cycle – why husbands do not love their wife and why their wives won't respect their husband. The second part of this book is about the energizing cycle – how husbands can love their wife and how wives can respect their husband. The third part is about the rewarded cycle – the real reason why both men and women should love and respect their spouses.

Chapter 1 – This talks about how love alone is not enough to make a marriage work. The simple secret to a happy marriage is respect.

Chapter 2 – Men and women hear and see things differently. This chapter talks about the coded message that men and women send to each other.

Chapter 3 – In this chapter, you'll learn why women do not respect their husbands and why husbands do not love their wives.

Chapter 4 – This chapter talks about why husband stonewall their wives.

Chapter 5 – In chapter 5, you'll learn how to break the cycle. Respecting your husband does not mean that you have to be a doormat.

Chapter 6 – This chapter encourages spouses to be mature enough to make the first move.

Chapter 7 – This chapter is about respect and how it can

motivate a man to love his wife.

Chapter 8 – This chapter is about the acronym COUPLE (closeness, openness, understanding, peacemaking, loyalty, and esteem).

Chapter 9 – This chapter talks about how important closeness is to women.

Chapter 10 – This is about how a husband can open up to his wife.

Chapter 11 – This chapter talks about how a husband can show his wife that he understands him.

Chapter 12 – This chapter is about the power of "I'm sorry".

Chapter 13 – This chapter is about how important loyalty is to women.

Chapter 14 – This is about how man can respect and honor his wife.

Chapter 15 – This chapter talks about how wives can get into the energizing cycle by understanding the acronym CHAIRS (Conquest, Hierarchy, Authority, Insight, Relationship, and Sexuality).

Chapter 16 – This talks about how a man values his work and how a woman can respect him by appreciating what he brings to the table.

Chapter 17 – This chapter is about the man's need to provide and protect his family. A wife should not belittle her husband's work.

Chapter 18 – This chapter talks about the husband's need to lead his family.

Chapter 19 – A woman must appreciate his desire to give advice to his wife.

Chapter 20 – This chapter is about the man's need to have a "shoulder to shoulder."

Chapter 21 – This chapter is about how important physical intimacy is to a husband.

Chapter 22 – This summarizes how both the husband and wife can get into the energizing cycle.

Chapter 23 – This is about the real reason why spouses should love and respect one another.

Chapter 24 – This chapter talks about the real reward of unconditional love and respect.

This book will help you cherish, value, and appreciate your spouse. What you are about to read is powerful enough to save your marriage.

## Introduction: Love Alone Is Not Enough

Do you want to be closer to your spouse? Do you want to achieve harmony in the household? Do you want to feel understood? Do you want to have a blissful marriage that's free of needless pain? Then, read this book.

The Beatles sang, "All you need is love." Well, that's not true at all.

Half of marriages end in divorce because love is simply not enough to keep a marriage going. Love is important, especially for women. However, what we all miss is the husband's need for respect. This book is about how the wife can fulfill her need to be loved by giving her husband the one thing that he needs – respect.

This book contains vital information that will help you save your marriage and build a deep relationship with your spouse. This book is for those who are going through marital problems. It is also for people who want to stay happily married until death. It is also for jaded divorcees, lonely wives, spouses who have been cheated, and engage couples. It is also for counselors and pastors who want to save marriages.

This book contains information that's powerful enough to

bring spouses closer to each other. However, what you are about to read is not a "miracle pill". Sometimes, the glow a spouse feels after reading this book fades in just a few weeks. They go back to the "crazy" cycle. You must practice the tips contained in this book for at least six weeks. This will help you make "respect" a part of your system. The quest for a happy and satisfying marriage is an ongoing process. It's never over.

If you're struggling with marriage, you should know that respect might be the missing piece of the puzzle. Read on to discover the power of respect.

# Part One: The Crazy Cycle

He reacts to her without love

She reacts to him without respect

The major problem of the wives is that they feel that their husband do not love them. You see, wives are made to expect, want, and make love. And many husbands fail to meet this vital need. After studying the scriptures and various books, Dr. Emerson Eggerichs found the other half of the equation.

Husbands do not complain much. Nevertheless, most of them have one concern – their wives do not respect them. This is the reason why fifty percent of marriages end in divorce. When a wife feels that her husband doesn't love her, she disrespects him. When a husband doesn't get respect from his wife, he acts without love. This cycle goes round and round. This is called the "crazy cycle". The first seven chapters of this book talks about the "crazy cycle" – what is it and how you can get out of it.

# 1. The Simple Secret to a Better Marriage

"How can I make my husband love me?" This is the most common question amongst wives during therapy and counseling. They weep and they're in deep pain. They do not know quite what to do. These women are so loving and tender. Dr. Emerson Eggerichs would empathize with these women and became irked with the husbands. Why can't these husbands see what they are doing to their wives?

Dr. Emerson Eggerichs came from an unhappy family. His parents would fight all the time and have separated (and reunited) a number of times. As he looked back, he knew the cause of the constant argument and conflict. His mom was crying for love while his father was craving for respect.

Dr. Emerson Eggerichs' mom taught dance and acrobatics. She was earning good money. She can survive without her husband. She constantly sends this message to her husband. She made financial decisions without asking for his opinion. This made him feel like he does not matter. Because he was hurt, he would act in unloving ways. He would get angry over small things. His mom is constantly heartbroken.

When he was in college, he met a lovely sanguine woman

named Sarah. She lights up every room she entered. She's loving and optimistic. Her parents got a divorce when she was young, but she moved on. She didn't have baggage. Dr. Emerson Eggerichs knew that she's the one.

### The Jean Jacket Disagreement

Dr. Emerson Eggerichs proposed to Sarah when they were still in college. She said yes. During their first Christmas as an engaged couple, she made him a lovely jean jacket. When Dr. Emerson Eggerichs saw the jacket, he said, "Thank you". Sarah said, "No, you don't like it because if you do, you will respond with enthusiasm".

At that time, Sarah felt unloved and Dr. Emerson Eggerichs felt disrespected. He felt as if he really didn't like who he is. That started the crazy cycle.

They were married in 1973 after Dr. Emerson Eggerichs graduated from Wheaton Graduate School. He started a Christian counseling center and he began to study the female and male differences.

Sarah is nurturing and she gets energized when she's with the people she cared about. Emerson, on the other hand, is analytical. One night, while they are driving home, Sara told her husband, "You were boring tonight at our bible study. You intimidate the people around you with your silence". That started the argument. Emerson felt like Sarah was putting him down. Sarah was already raising her voice.

Emerson knew that Sarah loved him and her outbursts were caused by her intense desire to help him improve his social skills. She wanted him to realize that she's doing everything she's doing out of love. She would constantly tell him what to do. Emerson would do his best to improve. However, he would slip every now and then. This would make Sarah feel that he did not value her opinion or input.

Then, one day, Emerson forgot Sarah's birthday. She was deeply hurt. Nevertheless, at the same time, Emerson felt like he has been put down. He felt disrespected. Feminism was in full blast during that time and men never talked about how they felt disrespected by women.

As years go by, Emerson and Sarah continued to have ups and downs in their marriage. She would criticize him and he would make excuses. He felt like he'll never be good enough, while Sarah felt that she was a failure as a mother and a wife.

Then, while after he earned the PHD, he realized that the secret to a happy marriage is in Ephesians 5:33 – "The husband must love his wife and the wife must respect her husband". That's when he realized the connection between love and respect.

*Love and Respect are Primary Needs*

Getting into a crazy cycle (lack of love, lack of respect) is easy. To have a happy marriage, it's necessary that spouses meet their need for love and respect.

You see, there's nothing as pure as a woman's love. When she loves you, she will go to the ends of the earth for you. A wife usually knows that her husband loves her, but she often asks if he loves her as much.

The husband also knows that his wife loves him. However, he frequently wonders if she likes him. When she's being critical, he misinterprets dislike as disrespect. He wants his wife's approval. When a husband gets angry, the wife feels unloved. When the woman nags her husband and tells him what to do, he feels disrespected.

Many books tell husbands to love their wives. This book introduces the concept of "unconditional respect" to the wives. This book will show you the power of "unconditional love" and "unconditional respect".

*Major Points:*

- ✓ The reason why most marriages end in divorce is the crazy cycle where the wife feels unloved and the husband feels disrespected.

- ✓ Wives want love. Husbands want respect.

## 2. To Communicate, Decipher the Code

To establish the love and respect the connection in your marriage, you must learn to read the messages that your spouse sends to you.

Let's look at a couple's story. This couple was about to celebrate their 10th anniversary. The wife was worried that her husband would not remember. He has forgotten their anniversary many times in the last ten years. However, surprisingly, he remembered. He went to Hallmark and got her the best card. He handed the card to her when she got home. She was happy. He finally remembered! She opened the card and she turned cold.

"What's wrong?" said the husband.

"Oh, it's nothing", the wife said.

"I can see that something's wrong".

"Well, it's a birthday card".

That started an intense argument. Most arguments are caused by the husband's carelessness. This makes the wife feel unloved. Then, the wife reacts with criticism, making the husband feel disrespected. Why would she respect him? That stupid man does not deserve respect!

Here's another example. The husband was gone for seven days on a business trip. When he got home, he envisioned a sexually-charged night with his wife. When he arrived home, the first words that came out of her wife's mouth was, "Oh, why are you here so early? Since you're here, why don't you pick up the kids at school and attend the parent-teacher meeting?"

The husband replied with a sarcastic tone. The wife was bothered by her husband's tone. But, she still has a lot of things to do. She could sense that he was angry. Later that night, she declined his sexual advances. This resulted in a fight. The wife finally aired out her sentiment, "You only remember me when you want sex".

Stories like these are more common than you think. This is the reason why divorce lawyers are laughing their way to the bank. These arguments happen because couples communicate in code, hoping that their partner will get the message.

Men and women send different messages. For example, when a woman says, "I have nothing to wear", it means that she has nothing new. When a man says, "I have nothing to wear", it means that he has no clean clothes. Men and women communicate differently and this is often the cause of the conflict.

### Men and Women Are As Different As Pink and Blue

Men look at things through blue glasses. Women, on the other hand, look at the world with rose pink glasses. Men and women see life situations differently. They also hear differently.

Let's take a look again at the "birthday" scenario. The husband gave the wife a birthday card during their anniversary. She thinks that her husband doesn't love her, so she sends him an angry message. Does he decipher the code correctly? No. All he can see is anger. He could not hear her cry for love. Her anger made him feel disrespected. After all, it was an honest mistake.

Because of their failure to decipher the spouse's message, husband and wife get into the crazy cycle (the cycle of lack of love and respect). They get into this cycle because they do not understand each other. They do not know that the issue at hand is not the real issue. The real issue is lack of love and respect.

As mentioned earlier, men and women hear differently. Women hear silence as hostility, while men hear criticism as anger and contempt.

*Major Points:*

✓ Men and women see and hear differently.

✓ Many marriages fail because the spouses are unable to decipher the codes sent by their partners.

✓ When your wife is crying, criticizing, and complaining, it means that she wants your love.

✓ When the husband is angry, hostile, or not speaking at all, he's sending a coded message that says, "I want your respect."

# 3. Why She Won't Respect; Why He Won't Love

Learning how to decipher your spouse's encoded message won't happen in a day or even a month. It's not as easy as you think.

## Unconditional Respect

Dr. Eggerichs talked to many wives. As it turns out, these wives do not have trouble understanding the concept of unconditional love. However, they have a hard time understanding the concept of unconditional respect. Wives believe that respect must be earned.

Nevertheless, what's interesting is that most husbands also don't understand the concept of unconditional respect. They also believe that respect must be earned. But, the wife generally thinks that her husband doesn't deserve respect. The husband wants to earn his wife's respect, and he believes that he doesn't deserve the disrespect that he's getting from her.

Most women get upset when they hear "unconditional respect." They would say, "If he loves me, then he gets my respect". They see "unconditional respect" as an oxymoron, the two words are contradictory. But, they don't see "unconditional love" as contradictory. Why? Well, it all goes back to the "pink and blue" concept that we discussed in the previous chapter.

You see, the church has stressed too much on the importance of unconditional love, but has not stressed the importance of unconditional respect.

Both men and women want love and respect. However, women's primary need is love, while men's primary need is respect. Aretha Franklin sang RESPECT, which suggests that women need respect, too. But, women usually feel respected when their husbands love them. Men, on the other hand, see respect differently.

Men understand the concept of "unconditional respect" because it is what they value the most. Men would rather be left alone and unloved than to be disrespected. For men, love is food and respect is water. If you want to motivate your husband, you have to respect him.

To illustrate how respect motivates men, let's look at the military. When a general respects his men and believes in them, the soldiers want to improve. These men want to serve and they are willing to die in a combat. Honor is important to men. The same honor and loyalty that drives a man to die for his general, motivates a man to die for his wife. **If his wife respects him, he will serve and love her**.

Nevertheless, the conflict often happens because men want their wives to respect them as the "head." Wives, on the other hand, do not want to be respected as the head. They simply want to be respected as "equals". A husband expects his wife to look up to him and yet, he puts his wife down.

When a husband honors his wife and treats her like an equal, she will respect him.

*Major Points:*

- ✓ Men need respect. Women need love.

- ✓ Men value respect more than love.

- ✓ Respect motivates a husband to serve and love his wife.

- ✓ To gain a woman's respect, the man must treat her as an equal.

# 4. What Men Fear Most Can Keep The Crazy Cycle Spinning

As mentioned earlier in this book, many men interpret nagging and criticism as contempt. Most men do not handle contempt very well. Women fear being unloved, while men fear disrespect.

Every woman would say that all she ever wanted is to be loved. She wanted someone who will make her feel special. Yet, no one accuses a woman of being a prima donna, diva, or an egomaniac when she says these words. However, when a man says that he wanted to be respected, people will say that he's arrogant.

During the courtship, the woman may think that it was her love that motivated the man to ask her to marry him. After all, she was motivated by love. Nevertheless, the truth is, what motivated him was her admiration. Man values admiration more than love. When a woman criticizes him, he withdraws because he thinks that it's the most honorable thing to do.

### Are You a Stonewaller or a Criticizer?

A research shows that a man would most likely stonewall his wife during an argument. This is because his blood pressure rises faster than his wife's. To calm himself down, he stonewalls. The wife usually sees stonewalling as unloving. She feels that he's rejecting her. Therefore, here's the cycle – she criticizes, he stonewalls, and then, she feels contempt for him. This puts the marriage in danger. This produces a vicious cycle that can lead to divorce.

The women are usually the criticizers and confronters. The husbands are the stonewallers. A few women stonewall their husbands and when they do, that's usually because they think that their husband do not have the ability to hear their heart.

A wife (who loves her husband deeply) will move towards him when he stonewalls her. For example, when he misses dinner without calling, she does what she thought as the most loving thing to do – tell her husband, "We need to talk". You see, this is how women approach their girlfriends to resolve conflicts. Most women think that this will work on their husbands.

A wife will fail to see the difference between her husband and her best friend. She's more judgmental towards her husband because she knows that she will always "outlove" him. Therefore, she will try to "change" him. However, when a wife tries to change her husband, her husband will close off because she's not making him feel good about himself. When a wife criticizes and confronts, she's trying to send the message "I need your love".

When a woman constantly nags her husband, he feels that he no longer looks up to him. He feels like he's putting him down. When the wife doesn't communicate using the "respect language", the husband is not interested in communicating with her at all.

When a husband receives unconditional respect from his wife, he will give the kind of love that she expects.

Nevertheless, here's the thing. Not all men are aware of their deep need for respect. They do not always articulate their intense need for respect.

### Are Love and Respect The Same?

A lot of wives say that love and respect are the same thing. However, they are not. For example, you respect your employer, but you don't love him. Wives need unconditional love, while husband needs unconditional respect.

*Major Points:*

- ✓ The woman criticizes. The man stonewalls.

- ✓ A man stonewalls during an argument to calm himself down.

- ✓ Men feel disrespected when their wives try to change them.

- ✓ A wife's nagging and scolding can start a crazy cycle.

- ✓ When a man feels that his wife no longer looks up to him, the crazy cycle begins.

- ✓ When a woman does not communicate with her husband using the "respect language", her husband will not want to communicate with her.

# 5. She Fears Being A Doormat; He's Tired of "Just Not Getting It"

Many wives still believe that respect must be earned. They are worried that they would end up being doormats. Most women think that they feel like they're a hypocrite if they would show respect to a man who doesn't deserve their respect.

## *Who Should Make The First Move?*

A woman must respect his husband. A husband must love his wife. However, who makes the first move? A wife would say, "I need your love before I can show you respect". Well, that would not work because when you say that, you are making your husband responsible for the entire marriage. When this happens, your husband will shut down.

The husband will also say that, "If my wife respects me, I will love her until eternity." So, let's go back to the question, who should make the first move? Well, the answer is, whoever is the more mature spouse.

## *Not a Doormat, But Women With Power*

Many women think that people who encourage unconditional respect are chauvinists. Respecting your husband is not the same thing as being a doormat. It does not mean that you should act stupid or curb your leadership abilities. The major goal is to break the cycle of negativity. Sadly, a lot of women feel empowered with negativity. They have this wrong notion that if they don't respect their husband, that means they are winning the battle. But, the truth is, it is them who are losing the war.

*Husbands, You Should Remember One Idea- Love*

Women always say that men don't get it. However, husbands should always realize that their wives have nothing but pure intentions. They are good-willed women. When they are being disrespectful, they are just begging for love. So, when a woman disrespects you, ask yourself if you've been unloving to her.

*Major Points:*

- ✓ To end the crazy cycle, the more emotionally mature spouse should make the move.

- ✓ Women do not respect their husbands because they are afraid of being a doormat.

- ✓ Respecting your husband does not mean that you act dumb or hide your leadership skills.

When women don't respect their husband, they feel empowered. They feel like they are winning the battle when, the truth is, they are losing the war.

# 6. She Worries About Being A Hypocrite; He Complains, "I Get No Respect"

There's this wife who has been married for more than thirty years. Her husband was a brave soldier who served in Vietnam. He was an overachiever. However, after he came back from the war, he became an alcoholic and he's unable to find a job. You could see why it's difficult for the wife to respect her husband. She said, "If I respect him even if he didn't earn it, I'll be a hypocrite".

A lot of wives feel the same way. Many women say, "If he feels disrespected, well that's his problem". Many wives attack, lecture, and criticize their husbands to win the battle. But, they are losing the war.

When a man is uncaring and unloving, the wife thinks that he should change. And he really should. The man must understand her need of being loved. But, the only way that she could get the love that she deserves is when she would respect her husband. Because he would feel that finally, his wife "gets it".

Remember this: <u>Showing respect even when you don't feel that your husband deserves it is a sign of maturity</u>. It's not hypocrisy.

To husbands who feel that they "get no respect". Don't give up. Be the mature one and show her that you love her. Do not withdraw from her.

Men and women should both humble themselves. Choose to be mature.

*Major Points:*

- ✓ Showing respect even when you feel that your husband doesn't deserve respect is not hypocrisy. It's a sign of maturity.

- ✓ When a husband feels disrespected, he should show his wife how much he loves her. Choose to conceal your dishonor. That's a sign of maturity.

## 7. She Thinks She Can't Forgive Him; He Says, "Nobody Can Love That Woman!"

A wife gets beaten down with her husband's harshness. She tried to forgive him, but he gets worse. Therefore, he disrespects him. And the cycle just keeps going. The problem is that only a few men will ask for forgiveness, especially if he feels disrespected.

Dr. Eggrichs agrees that it's not fair to ask wives to forgive their cold and unforgiving husbands. Nevertheless, to start a cycle of love and respect, the wife must learn to forgive her husband. Yes, your husband's action may have hurt you, but you should not retaliate by offending and disrespecting him.

Remember that Jesus said, "He who has no sin, should be the first one to throw the rock at her". You should be mature enough to forgive your husband. Jesus said, "Do not judge and you will not be judged".

A man, on the other hand, thinks, "How could anyone love someone as disrespectful as his wife?" To stop the cycle, the husband must also love his wife even if he's not unlovable at the moment. That's the only way that a marriage will work.

*Marriage: Two Become One*

For the marriage to work, both spouses must carry the load. Both spouses must try to love and respect each other. When this happens – the energizing cycle begins.

Remember that her respect motivates his love and his love motivates her respect.

*Major Points:*

- ✓ The woman must forgive her husband. She must avoid judging him.

- ✓ The man must be matured enough to love his wife even when she's disrespectful.

- ✓ A woman's respect motivates a man's love. A man's love motivates a woman's respect.

# Part Two: The Energizing Cycle

His love motivates her respect

Her respect motivates his love

To stop the crazy cycle from spinning, you and your spouse must get to the Energizing Cycle. The next chapters are about the important passages in the bible that strengthens the love and respect connection in a marriage. You could also find techniques, principles, and easy to follow tips that husbands and wives can easily follow.

The next chapters also contain advice for husbands that are symbolized by the acronym COUPLE: Closeness, Openness, Understanding, Peace-making, Loyalty, and Esteem. The advice for wives is covered by the acronym CHAIRS: Conquest, Hierarchy, Authority, Insight, Relationship, and Sexuality.

It takes constant work to get into the energizing cycle and in that cycle.

## 8. C-O-U-P-L-E: How to Spell Love to Your Wife

To step out of the crazy cycle, husbands must learn to be the mature one. If you want your wife to treat you with respect, you have to treat your wife with love and you can do this by understanding the acronym called COUPLE. This will energize your wife and inspire her to respect you.

Most men think that their wife is trying to control them. It's not true. When she's nagging or acting in a disrespectful way, she is crying for love. To get into the energizing cycle, the husband must give his wife what she needs the most – closeness, openness, understanding, peacemaking, loyalty, and esteem.

The next chapters talk about how husbands could love his wife and gain her respect.

# 9. Closeness – She Wants You To Be Close

Women have the desire to be close to her husband. Your wife will feel loved when you move closer to her. Touch her and smile at her often. You see, a wife has a strong desire to connect. After a long day, you just want to relax and sit in front of the TV. However, this uninvolved behavior will make your wife feel neglected and unloved. Instead of sitting in front of the TV, help your wife prepare dinner. Talk to her and ask her about her day. Tell her about your day.

Some men do not want to be close to their wives because they want to maintain their independence. In addition, most men do want to initiate closeness, unless they feel their wife's respect. Nevertheless, if you want your wife to respect you, you must spend time with her. You must be affectionate without wanting sex. Just touch her, hold her hand, and hug her often.

*To be closer to your wife, you must follow these tips:*

- ✓ Do something with your wife – you can walk, jog, or just laugh together.

- ✓ Set a date night every week.

✓ Run an errand for her.

✓ Make her your priority. Spend time with her.

✓ Talk to her after sex. Engage in a pillow talk.

## 10. Openness – She Wants You To Open Up to Her

As mentioned earlier in this book, men and women see things in a different way. Men see blue. Women see pink. They also hear words differently. To build a happy marriage, you must learn to decode your wife's message. You must learn to read your wife's emotions and see her crushed spirit. Her face tells it all.

When your wife complains, do not say, "Let's just move on and forget about it". Let her open up to you and take time to share your thoughts with her. Talk it out.

During the courtship stage, both men and women are open to each other. They share each other's dreams, fears, and even failures. So, why do men shut down after marriage? Well, the man thinks that his dream of marrying her was already fulfilled, so he does not see the need to open up to her. He now wants a "shoulder to shoulder" relationship with her where there's no need to talk about emotions or dreams.

Women are different. They are sensitive. They need their husbands to open to them. They need to hear their husband's thoughts, dreams, and aspirations on a regular basis. If you will fulfill her need for openness, you will get her respect.

*Here's a list of tips that you can use to be more open to your wife:*

✓ Listen to her. Ask for her opinion.

✓ Share your feelings – your dreams, problems, and difficulties. After all, your wife is your partner.

✓ Maintain a good eye contact while you talk to her.

✓ Pray with your wife.

✓ Discuss your work and future plans with your wife.

# 11. Understanding – Don't Try to Fix Her; Just Listen

The thing about most men is that they think that they are the stronger sex. This is the reason why they try to fix their wife and her problems. However, your wife will feel like you don't understand her if you try to "fix" her.

Your wife feels vulnerable and hurt when:

1.  You say, "I don't understand you" or "Is this worth the try?"

2.  You dishonor her by treating her as your subordinate and not your equal.

Feminists often say that the bible views women as the weaker sex. That's not true. The phrase in the bible that says a woman is a "weaker vessel" simply illustrates the difference between men and women. Think of two bowls – one is made of porcelain while the other one is made of copper. The porcelain bowl is more fragile and delicate, but it does not mean that it's less valuable than the copper one.

To have a happy marriage, you must treat your wife as an equal. Just listen to your wife when she talks about her problem. Do not suggest a solution. She doesn't need you to fix the problem; she just needs someone to talk to.

*These tips will make your wife feel that you truly understand her:*

- ✓ When your wife talks to you about her personal struggles, say "I really appreciate that you are sharing that with me."

- ✓ Do not interrupt her when she's talking.

- ✓ Listen actively and try to repeat what she's said. This will assure her that you understand what she's saying.

- ✓ Cut her some slack when she's having her period.

- ✓ Pray with her regularly.

- ✓ Pray for her.

- ✓ Apologize when you're wrong. Do not be afraid to admit your mistakes.

- ✓ Do not dismiss her feelings.

## 12. Peace-making – She Wants You To Say "I'm Sorry"

You won't have a happy marriage unless there's peace. There's one husband who tried to motivate his wife to respect him by being harsh to her. It didn't work. You see, you can't fully connect with your wife if you're constantly in conflict with her. You must make an effort to make peace with her.

Most men complain that their spouse can get a little historical. Wives usually bring up past mistakes during an argument and this can be frustrating. This is the reason why husbands try to end the argument by saying, "Let's just drop it".

*Why It's Hard For Men To Say "I'm Sorry"*

Many men do not say, "I'm Sorry" because they think that it's a sign of weakness. They are afraid that they will lose respect when they do so.

Many husbands also think that "I'm sorry" are just words. So, why both, right? However, you have to understand that words are intensely powerful to your wife. Saying "I'm sorry" will make her trust you more. It can lead to peace and healing.

Saying "I'm sorry" can be hard, but it's worth it. When you genuinely say, "I'm sorry", you will touch your wife's spirit.

*Follow these tips to promote peace in your home:*

- ✓ Let your wife vent. Do not get angry.

- ✓ Do not close off during an argument.

- ✓ Forgive your wife when she asks for forgiveness.

- ✓ Do not nurture your bitterness.

- ✓ You have to assure your wife of your love.

- ✓ Pray with your wife after resolving a conflict.

- ✓ Do not say, "Forget it".

- ✓ Admit your mistakes by saying, "I'm sorry".

# 13. Loyalty – She Needs to Know That You're Committed

Women constantly need reassurance of their husband's love. You see, women are generally loyal. They are committed to their husbands. However, she constantly wonders if her husband is loyal to her. It's difficult to be a wife in today's porn-laden world. Nevertheless, there's more to loyalty than not cheating on your wife.

Loyalty is about staying with your wife no matter what (even when she's sick or have gained weight). Most women stand by their husbands no matter what. However, only a few men will stand by his wife when she gets sick or when she gain extra pounds.

*Assure your wife of your loyalty by following these tips:*

- ✓ Speak highly of wife when you're talking to your friends and family.

- ✓ Do not correct her or put her down in front of your children.

- ✓ Avoid looking lustfully at other women.

- ✓ Do not flirt with other women.

✓ Tell your kids, "Do not ever talk to your mother that way!" if you hear them talking back.

✓ Assure your wife that you will be with her no matter what.

✓ Speak positively of your wife in front of others.

## 14. Esteem – She wants you to Honor and Cherish Her

Women need to be respected and esteem. To get your wife's respect, you must also respect her. You should not make your wife feel as if she's a failure.

As a husband, your self-image is usually tied to your work. However, your wife ties her self-worth to her family. A female CEO of an airline company once said that at the end of the day, there's nothing that she wants more than her husband's love and respect.

Women are the ones who gave birth to babies. This is the reason why birthdays are important to her. If you get her a good gift, you're honoring and cherishing her. You don't have to get her something expensive. But, make sure to put a lot of thought in your gifts.

*Here's how you can make your feel esteemed:*

- ✓ How the door for her.

- ✓ Speak highly of her in front of your friends, family, and co-workers.

- ✓ Don't forget to give her gifts during special occasions. You don't have to give her something expensive.

- ✓ Prioritize family outings over time with your friends.

- ✓ Teach others to respect her.

- ✓ Tell her how proud you are of what she does.

- ✓ Tell her how important she is.

# 15. CHAIRS: How to Spell Respect To Your Husband

In the last few chapters, we've discussed how husbands can love their wives. The next chapters are about how wives can show respect to their husbands. The next chapter is about the acronym C-H-A-I-R-S (Conquest, Hierarchy, Authority, Insight, Relationship, and Sexuality).

As mentioned in Proverbs 14:1, a wise woman builds her house, but a foolish woman tears her house down.

In Conquest, you will learn how to appreciate your husband's work and desire to achieve. In Hierarchy, you will learn how to appreciate what he provides. Authority is about appreciating his inner desire to lead and serve. Insight is about appreciating his need to counsel and give advice. Relationship is about understanding his need for friendship. Sexuality explains his deep need for sexual intimacy.

Unconditional respect is still an alien concept to most women. So, to get into the energizing cycle, you must use the "respect test" on your husband.

*The Respect Test*

Here's what you should do, you should stop and talk about the things that you respected about your husband. Then, go

140

to your husband and while he's busy or distracted, tell him "I just want you to know that I respect you. There are a lot of things that I respect about you". Now, don't wait for a response. Your husband will most likely scream, "Wait, what things?" After you say what you respect about him, he will most likely to ask you out to have dinner with him. This would surprise you because your husband rarely takes you out for dinner. She honored him and he wants to do something about it.

So, is this manipulation? Can a wife manipulate her husband into taking her on a cruise? Well, this is not manipulation. You are sincerely expressing your respect for your husband. You are just acknowledging your husband's intention to serve his family.

Nevertheless, you must be aware that some men may take a while before they respond to this test and that's okay.

*Be Ready With The Reasons Why You Respect Him*

When you do the respect test, you must be ready with the reasons why you respect him. You can say, "Honey, I appreciate how you go to work every day so you could provide for the family". The key is to focus on the positive and not on the negative. Remember that when your husband is angry, he doesn't want to hurt you. He was just starving for respect. A man has the need to be in the driver's seat. He wants to take control. He wants to be the first of equals.

Dale Carnegie once said that respect is the bedrock of motivation. In the next chapters, you will learn how you can motivate your husband to love you even more.

*Major Points:*

- ✓ To motivate your husband to love you, you must do the Respect Test. Tell your husband the reasons why you respect him and he would want to give the world to you.

- ✓ As a wife, you must understand the acronym CHAIRS (conquest, hierarchy, authority, insight, relationship, sexuality)

- ✓ Always remember the acronym CHAIRS: Conquest, Hierarchy, Authority, Insight, Relationship, and Sexuality.

- ✓ CHAIRS = Conquest, Hierarchy, Authority, Insight, Relationship, and Sexuality.

# 16. Conquest – Appreciate His Desire To Work And Achieve

Conquest is often associated with the dark ages where men think that it is their birthright to conquer a woman – emotionally, mentally, sexually, and physically. However, that's not the kind of conquest we're talking about here. Conquest is the natural desire of men to achieve and work. As a wife, you have to understand how important it is for a man to achieve something great.

To illustrate this point, let's take a look at a story. The husband lost his job. He came home and he looks lost and defeated. Therefore, his wife comforted him and said, "It's okay, as long as we have each other". She noticed that her husband is distancing himself from her. The wife could not understand why.

Here's the reason why saying "It's okay, honey, we have each other" doesn't work. Your husband is secured in your love. He doesn't need reassurance. Nevertheless, his work is something that's part of who he is. When he loses his job, he'll also lose a part of his identity.

When a man meets another man, the first question he asks is "What do you do?" You see, men feel that their work is part of who they are. A husband is a hunter, doer, and a worker. He wants a woman who believes in him. Remember Proverbs 12:4 NIV, a wife's noble character is the husband's crown.

To establish a happy marriage, you should support your husband's need for conquest. You should appreciate all the work that he does. You should not treat him as if he's just a meal ticket.

*Here's how you can show your husband that you appreciate his strong desire to work and achieve:*

- ✓ Tell him that you appreciate his effort to work.

- ✓ Express your faith in him.

- ✓ Listen to his stories about his work.

- ✓ See yourself as a partner.

- ✓ Do not criticize his work.

*Major Points:*

- ✓ Men believe that their work is a part of their identity.

- ✓ A man wants a woman who believes in him.

- ✓ Do not criticize his work.

# 17. Hierarchy: Appreciate His Desire To Protect and Provide

For years, men have used the scripture to dominate and abuse women. They have justified their terrible treatment of women by saying, "I told you so."

However, the Bible does not say that men should treat women as inferior. By hierarchy, Dr. Emerson means that men have a strong desire to lead. They have the instinct to provide.

*The Seven Words That Will Deflate The Husband*

Here's a story. A married couple was invited into their friends' home. The house was beautiful. It has lovely furniture and granite countertops. Then, the wife said the seven words that most men dread, "You need to get a second job". The husband's spirit fell down instantly. The sad part about this story is that the wife has not realized what she had done. She didn't know that she was disrespectful. She didn't know how much she broke her husband's heart.

*To build a happy marriage, you must appreciate your husband's desire and effort to protect and provide by following these tips:*

✓ Tell your husband how much you admire him.

- ✓ Praise your husband's commitment to provide for your family.

- ✓ If you don't want your husband to look down on you, you must look up to him.

- ✓ Do not demoralize your man, even when he can't provide much. Be prepared to light the candle when the electricity gets cut off.

*Major Points:*

- ✓ Wives should respect their husband's need to provide.

- ✓ You should never tell your husband to get a second job.

- ✓ Show respect by sticking with your husband even during tough times.

- ✓ Do not belittle your husband's work.

## 18. Authority: Appreciate His Desire To Serve and to Lead

In today's feminist world, we're constantly asking, "Who's the boss at home?" Many women feel that they are smarter than their husbands, that they should be the boss. However, according to the bible, husbands are primarily responsible to make the major decisions in a household. Does this mean that the wife must submit to his husband's decision even if he's doing something that's immoral or illegal? Should a wife submit to his husband even if he's deceitful and dishonest? The answer is no. If the man acts in an immoral, adulterous, and deceitful ways, he forfeits his right to "lead" his family.

Even if the husband is recognized as the head of the family, both spouses must mutually submit to each other. Nevertheless, if someone has to call the shots, it must be the husband. What if the wife disagrees with the husband's decision? Well, the wife must distance herself from her husband. She should not lecture or criticize him. The wife's quiet and respectful behavior will be a magnet. It would encourage the husband to love her and cherish her.

Is this an anti-feminist advice? No. This advice simply tells you how to get what you want from your husband by giving

147

him what he wants – _respect_. Your respectful behavior will surely win him over.

_To recognize your husband's need to lead, you need to follow these tips:_

- ✓ Tell your husband how strong you think he is.

- ✓ Be gracious, even if he makes a bad decision. Do not say, "I told you so".

- ✓ Praise him when he makes good decisions.

- ✓ Build his image as the leader of your household.

- ✓ Do not play mind games with your husband. Be the loving peacemaker.

_Major Points:_

- ✓ The wife must recognize her husband as the head of the family.

- ✓ The wife must submit, but she must not submit blindly. A man who acts in a dishonest, immoral, and adulterous ways forfeits his right as the leader of the family.

- ✓ The wife and the husband must mutually submit to one another.

# 19. Insight: Appreciate His Desire to Analyze and Counsel

The husband has the need to counsel and analyze so it is important that you honor this need. You should respect him by listening to his insights.

*To honor his need to counsel and analyze, follow these tips:*

- ✓ Take time to recognize your husband's problem-solving approach.

- ✓ Let your husband "fix" things and applaud him for doing so.

- ✓ Respect your husband even when his opinion is different from yours.

- ✓ Thank your husband for his advice.

- ✓ See your husband as a wise man.

## 20. Relationship: Appreciate His Desire For Shoulder to Shoulder Friendship

A couple has been married for seven years and they would engage in huge fights more frequently. The woman is usually in the kitchen and the husband is watching TV. He would call her and ask her to watch TV with him. She thinks that sitting in front of the TV is a waste of time, so she started to talk. The husband says, "I do not want to talk. I just want you to be with me". This eventually leads to a huge fight.

You see, this is how men share their experiences to other people. Women talk about their experiences. Men share their experiences with their wife by sharing an activity with her. Men prefer "shoulder-to-shoulder" friendship that does not require talking. Men do not hear words, they hear action.

*To fulfill a man's need for shoulder-to-shoulder friendship, you must follow these tips:*

- ✓ You should do fun activities with your husband like watching TV or some kind of sports.

- ✓ Encourage your husband to spend time alone. This energizes him to spend more time with you later.

- ✓ Respect his friends.

## 21. Sexuality: Appreciate His Desire for Sexual Intimacy

A doctor and his wife are on a crazy cycle. Their marriage was not a happy one. The problem was caused by the wife's ultimatum. She would not fulfill his sexual needs unless he fulfills her emotional needs. After all, that's what love is, right? One day, the wife decided to fulfill her husband's sexual need. And at that money, her husband started to fulfill her emotional needs. A man feels loved when he is physically intimate with his wife. When a wife refuses his need for sexual release, he feels like his wife does not care about his needs.

A man's need for physical release is the same as a woman's emotional release. It brings him satisfaction. This may hard to accept, but men are lured into extra-marital affairs because he's sexually deprived at home.

### A Dose of Respect Beats A Dose of Viagra

If you feel like you're husband is withdrawing from you sexually, you should try to respect him. Respect beats Viagra anytime. When you respect him, he would feel sexually closer to you.

*Here's how you can respect your husband's need for sexual intimacy:*

✓ You must initiate sex more often.

✓ Do not look at sex as a responsibility, you must genuinely enjoy it.

✓ Do not deprive him of sex to get him to do what you want.

# 22. The Energizing Cycle Will Work If You Do

To get into the energizing cycle, both spouses should be committed in making the marriage work.

Husbands should ask these COUPLE questions regularly:

1.  Closeness – Do I move toward her constantly? Do I spend time with my wife?

2.  Openness – Do I share my deepest thoughts and dreams with my wife?

3.  Understanding – Do I try not to fix her problems? Do I try to understand her emotions?

4.  Peacemaking – Am I ready to swallow my pride and resolve the issues?

5.  Loyalty – Do I constantly assure her that I will be loyal to her forever?

6.  Esteem – Do I tell my wife that I treasure her?

Wives could learn how to show respect to their husbands by asking these CHAIRS questions regularly:

1.  Conquest – Do I support and appreciate my husband's work?

2. Hierarchy – Do I respect my husband's need to provide and protect the family?

3. Authority – Do I respect my husband as the leader of our family?

4. Insight – Do I ask for my husband's opinion?

5. Relationship – Do I spend time with my husband? Do I like doing activities with him?

6. Sexuality – Do I recognize my husband's need for physical release?

When the couple goes into the energizing cycle, they will experience marital bliss. They will love, respect, and support each other.

In the next part of this book, we will discuss the "rewarded cycle." This cycle helps you to develop your maturity and to win your spouse over.

## Part Three: The Rewarded Cycle

The husband loves his wife, despite her respect

The wife respects her husband, despite his love

To get love, the wife must respect her husband. To get respect, the husband must love his wife. But, if you want a lasting and blissful marriage, both the husband and the wife should respect and love each other no matter what. This means that the husband must love the wife, despite her respect. The wife must respect her husband, despite his love.

## 23. The Real Reason to Love and Respect

Many couples refuse to practice the love and respect connection because they are afraid that it would not work. And the truth is sometimes, it doesn't. Sometimes, a wife will not get love even when she respects her husband. Sometimes, a husband will not get respect even if he loves his wife. So, what should you do if it doesn't work? Well, the answer is to get into the rewarded cycle. The husband must love his wife, regardless of her respect. The wife must respect her husband, regardless of his love.

The bible says, "Do not pay unkind words with unkind words. When someone says unkind words to you, respond with kind words."

The real reason to love and respect your spouse is to get the heaven's blessing. If a wife respects her unloving husband, she will get eternal blessing.

It may not make sense for a wife to respect her harsh and unloving husband. It may not make sense for the husband to love his disrespectful wife. However, this makes sense to God and He rewards spouses who give their partners unconditional love and respect.

A wife's unconditional respect for her husband is a sign of her reverence for God. A husband's unconditional love for his wife is a sign of his love for God.

Remember that, in the ultimate sense, your marriage has really nothing to do with your spouse. It has everything to do with your relationship with God.

## 24. The Truth Can Make You Free, Indeed

Marriage is really a test of your unconditional love for your spouse. It is also a test of your desire to please and honor God. When you try to do this more often, you will meet your needs. However, you must remember that the first goal is to obey and please God.

Remember that it's okay to get hurt with your spouse's actions, but choose peace instead of hatred and contempt. When you do this, you'll earn the reward from heavens – you will experience inner freedom.

Inner freedom helps you build a legacy. Your children will look up to you.

What do you want your children to think of you? What do you want your children to say at your funeral? So, choose to be the mature one and you will be rewarded with legacy of being a good spouse. You will be blessed by the heavens.

# Conclusion: Pink and Blue Can Make God's Purple

As mentioned throughout the book, men and women think, see, and hear differently. Women see pink and men see blue. Because the husband and the wife see things differently, this can result to the "Crazy Cycle" – the love, there's no respect; without respect, there's no love.

To get out of the Crazy Cycle – the husband must love his wife to get her respect; the wife must respect her husband to get love.

Nevertheless, what if love and respect doesn't work? Well, you should still strive to respect and love your spouse regardless of his/her love and respect for you. You will be rewarded with inner freedom and you will create your own legacy.

Also, make sure to pray. Prayer is a powerful tool that you can use to build a happy marriage. After all, Christ is the center of all marriages.

*Here's a list of the major points of this book:*

- ✓ Love is not enough for a marriage to work.
- ✓ Love is important, especially to women. However, there's nothing that men crave more than respect.

- ✓ The love and respect connection is the secret to a happy marriage.

- ✓ Most couples are in the crazy cycle where husbands do not love their wife and wives do not respect their husbands.

- ✓ Men and women see, think, and hear differently. Men see blue while women see pink.

- ✓ The wife and the husband communicate to their spouse in codes.

- ✓ The concept of unconditional respect is something that a lot of women can't understand. Women believe that respect must be earned.

- ✓ Men value respect more than love. They are craving for unconditional respect.

- ✓ To gain a man's love, you must respect him.

To gain a woman's respect, you must love and cherish her.

✓ When a woman is nagging, she's crying for love.

✓ When a man is harsh, he's crying for respect.

✓ Women do not respect their husband because they don't want to be a doormat.

✓ A man's identity is tied to his work. A woman's identity is tied to her family.

*Here's how a man could show his love for his wife:*

✓ Move close to her and spend more time with her.

✓ Appreciate everything that she does for the family.

✓ Set a date night weekly.

✓ Be proud of her.

✓ Thank her for taking care of you and your kids.

✓ Honor your wife.

- ✓ Praise her cooking.

- ✓ Protect her good name and reputation.

- ✓ Move towards her and ask her about her day.

- ✓ Run an errand for your wife every now and then.

- ✓ Encourage your kids to respect your wife.

- ✓ Do not shut her down when she's trying to communicate her feelings.

- ✓ Listen to your wife and ask for your opinion.

- ✓ Share your feelings, problems, and dreams to your wife.

- ✓ Allow your wife to vent. Do not just say, "Let's forget about it". Do not dismiss her concerns.

- ✓ Do not close off.

- ✓ Do not stonewall your wife, especially when you're frustrated or you feel disrespected.

- ✓ Assure your wife that you are loyal to her.

- ✓ Avoid flirting with another woman. That's disrespectful to your wife.

- ✓ Speak highly of your wife, especially in front of others.

*Here's how a woman can show her respect for her husband:*
- ✓ Tell him how much you respect him.

- ✓ Tell him how much you admire him.

- ✓ Appreciate your husband's need to work and succeed.

- ✓ Do not criticize your husband's work.

- ✓ Do not undermine your husband's authority.

- ✓ Tell him why you admire him.

- ✓ Give sincere compliments.

- ✓ Avoid criticizing your husband, especially in front of other people.

- ✓ Focus on what your husband is doing right.

- ✓ Touch him.

- ✓ Thank your husband for working to provide for your family.

- ✓ Take care of yourself and your appearance.

- ✓ Forgive him.

- ✓ Smile at him more often.

- ✓ Tell your husband that you believe in him, that you have faith in him.

- ✓ Do not belittle your husband's work.

- ✓ Appreciate what your husband can provide.

- ✓ Tell your husband how much you appreciate all the work that he does for your family.

- ✓ Build your husband's self-image as the leader of your family.

- ✓ Do fun activities with your husband to fulfill his need for "shoulder to shoulder" friendship.

- ✓ Initiate sex often.

- ✓ Do not dismiss your husband's need for physical intimacy.

- ✓ Speak highly of your husband when you're talking to him.

- ✓ You must recognize your husband's need as the head of the family.

- ✓ You must give your husband unconditional respect. You should respect him even if you feel that he doesn't deserve your respect.

- ✓ Respect his friends.

- ✓ Respect your husband's independence. Give him freedom, so he would have a strong desire to connect with you.

Most of all, remember that when you give your spouse unconditional love and respect, you're obeying God's will.

I hope that you use the tips and strategies contained in this book to improve your marriage and give you the happiness that you crave.

## Food for thought…

It takes two to tango. To make a marriage work, the wife must respect her husband and the husband must respect his wife. They should work as a team.

It's not easy. However, a husband must fulfill the emotional needs of his wife. He must listen to her and let her vent. He must be loyal to her. He must tell her his dreams, hopes, problems, and challenges.

The wife must also learn the concept of unconditional respect. She must appreciate her husband's work. She must think highly of him and value his input. She must see him as the leader of the family.

Love makes the world go round. However, fifty percent of marriages end in divorce because love alone is not enough and respect is the missing part of the puzzle. It's the secret to a happy and blissful marriage.

## Final Thoughts

Hey! Did you enjoy this book? We sincerely hope you thoroughly enjoyed this short read and have gotten immensely valuable insights that will help you in any areas of your life.

Would it be too greedy if we ask for a review from you?

It takes 1 minute to leave 1 review to possibly influence 1 more person's decision to read just 1 book which may change their 1 life. Your 1 minute matters and we value it and thank you so much for giving us your 1 minute. If it sucks, just say it sucks. Period.

# FREE BONUS

**P.S. Is it okay if we overdeliver?**

Here at Abbey Beathan Publishing, we believe in overdelivering way beyond our reader's expectations. Is it okay if we overdeliver?

Here's the deal, we're going to give you an extremely valuable cheatsheet of "Accelerated Learning". We've partnered up with Ikigai Publishing to present to you the exclusive bonus of "Accelerated Learning Cheatsheet"

What's the catch? We need to trust you... You see, we want to overdeliver and in order for us to do that, we've to trust our reader to keep this bonus a secret to themselves. Why? Because we don't want people to be getting our exclusive accelerated learning cheatsheet without even buying our books itself. Unethical, right?

Ok. Are you ready?

Simply Visit this link: http://bit.ly/acceleratedcheatsheet

We hope you'll enjoy our free bonuses as much as we've enjoyed preparing it for you!

# Free Bonus #2: Free Book Preview of Summary: Jab, Jab, Jab, Right Hook

## The Book at a Glance

Gary Vaynerchuk likens doing business to boxing. The way a boxing match goes is closely similar to how businesses and consumers interact with each other. In the modern setting, of which social media marketing is an essential part, businesses jab their consumers by providing content that can entertain and inform. Depending on how the consumers respond, the business can then proceed to jab some more or go for a right hook, which is equated to the sale or closing of the deal. This engagement is what Gary believes to be the driving force between business-consumer interaction online and offline.

In this book, Gary intends to educate businesses and marketers, especially those with small businesses, in the way of social media marketing. With his expertise and experience from his own success and his clients' from VaynerMedia, he hopes to teach the reader how to succeed in getting their brand known by their target audience. In doing so, the reader will hopefully be able to capitalize and create results from effective offers and promotions done on social media platforms.

The first few chapters of this book delve on the current set-up of the world regarding use of mobile devices and social media networks. The progress of this evolution in media has happened in the same way in previous forms, particularly in print, radio, and television. He also iterates how the modern story-telling process works in marketing and how it was shaped to its current form by social media. Then, he enumerates valuable pointers on how to create valuable content that will be effective jabs to make your audience relate with your brand.

In the next part, he builds upon the characteristics of good content to provide insight on current best practices and effective marketing strategies on the most used social media platforms. Facebook, Twitter, Pinterest, Instagram, and Tumblr are tackled individually. For each of these platforms, the right kind of content is explained and some tips are given on how to create effective content native to the platform. He also explores the opportunities from some of the emerging social media networks.

Transitioning from the different social media platforms, he explains the importance of effort to achieve success in any area of life. He says that it is true that small businesses have a great disadvantage when it comes to resources. This greatly affects their capability to match the marketing efforts of bigger businesses. However, the disadvantage of being a small organization is an advantage in of itself as it enables such businesses to respond at a faster rate to their audience's needs, interests, and preferences. He reiterates that, depending on the quality of effort exerted, advantages such as capital, budget, and human resource can be overcome.

In the last part, he states that the requirements for success in the modern day are a lot more different than those in the past. This is mostly due to the technological and socio-cultural changes brought on by various modern advancements. More changes will occur and things will get more difficult. Nevertheless, in the scheme of things, this shouldn't be the problem if your mindset is that of constant learning and development to achieve and maintain the leading position. Having this mindset will equip you to always fight for that position and, in the process, you will constantly grow as a professional.

# Introduction: Weigh in

Business, like boxing, has an aggressive, competitive, and fast-paced feel to it. This is no different in the world of social media marketing. Companies create big campaigns or promotions to create results that will give them advantage over their competition. Like the right hooks in boxing, they know that these events deliver sales and the return of investment for their business.

In the current setting, marketers create campaigns one after the other but they still fail in creating the results they are after. This failure is borne out of the assumption that, with a well-executed right hook, one can lessen or forego creating relationships with their customers. It would have worked in the age of television and digital media; however, social media has changed the dynamics of business-customer interaction.

Frequent and numerous promotional offers just do not work as much anymore as today's business; like boxing, it does not consist only of right hooks. Yes, often, only the right hook is seen as the punch that won the match. However, without the boxer (the business) delivering jabs (customer engagement), the delivery of the "right hook" would surely miss. Either the recipient of such promotions would ignore it or it will have no audience at all as it did not provide the requisite jabs for customer engagement.

The inspiration for this book came from the realization that Gary's success for Wine Library TV was a result of authentic and genuine content suited for YouTube. The author emphasized in his previous book, *The Thank You Economy*, and in his various speaking engagements that social media marketing should be done with the long-term in mind. There should be genuine and solid customer engagement as this will create active and real relationships with one's customers. However, as Gary realized, sales and return on investment cannot be achieved by only using customer engagement. There should be well-executed "right hooks", or campaigns and sales as well, to create the revenue that will spell success for the business.

In his first book, *Crush It!*, Gary taught the readers how to create great content and how to utilize content for the different platforms available at that time. Nevertheless, the changes in existing platforms and development of new ones have brought about the need to change past approaches to deliver successful right hooks in the current setting. With this book, all the knowledge from the first two books will be updated and combined to illustrate how to apply it in the current social media and digital environment.

Regardless of the type of company or organization you're in, your task is to tell the story of your organization, company, or brand to your customer. Especially now that what was done in print, radio, and television has a smaller audience as to what it used to before, and direct e-mails and banner ads are not as effective as before. The only option for the most effective marketing is through social media as this is where people spend most of their time now.

This book will set you up in how to tell your story on the most important social media platforms of the time. The storytelling formula will be taught to you so that your story will be effective delivering your message to your customers. An examination of some of the good, bad, and ugly stories done by different companies will be done to illustrate the common pitfalls in social media marketing. Once you've learn all this book can teach, you will be able to adapt to any new platforms in the future.

*Jab, Jab, Jab, Right Hook* is considered to be the last book in Gary Vaynerchuk's trilogy on the evolution of social media and of his career as a marketer and businessman. Although the world and the available platforms change, the secret to creating results remains the same. To attain brand awareness and profit through social media marketing, it requires the classic and everlasting values of hard work, passion, constant engagement, sincerity, long-term commitment, and clever and strategic storytelling.